GOD TRAUMA AND
WISDOM THERAPY

GOD TRAUMA AND WISDOM THERAPY

A COMMENTARY ON JOB

NORMAN C. HABEL

FORTRESS PRESS
Minneapolis

Library of Congress Control Number: 2023025619 (print)

Cover design: Laurie Ingram
Cover art: William Blake, Head of Job, c. 1825 (Fitzwilliam Museum,
Cambridge, UK).

Print ISBN: 978-1-5064-9929-1
eBook ISBN: 978-1-5064-9930-7

Printed in China.

CONTENTS

II
Wisdom Therapy
Job 28–42

PREFACE

A few days before Christmas in 1953, my brother and I were playing tennis a few miles from home. A lady who lived next to the tennis court received a phone call. Our home was on fire.

We drove our old buckboard home as fast as it could go. When we arrived, our weatherboard home had become one mass of flames. There was no chance of getting inside. Everything was burning—our beds, our clothes, our books, and our memories.

My mother stood watching in silence, her heart completely broken and unable to pronounce one of her favorite lines, "Thy will be done."

As people drove down the country road in front of our house, they stopped and watched in amazement at the fury of the flames. After a while, the pious Lutheran pastor from our nearby town arrived with my father who had been helping in a working bee at the church.

The Lutheran pastor came up behind me, put his hand on my shoulder, presumably to console me, and quoted from the book of Job, saying,

> *Norman,*
> *The Lord giveth and the Lord taketh away.*
> *Blessed be the name of the Lord.*

How insensitive! Why on Earth would I want to bless the name of the Lord when I was faced with the destruction of everything I owned and loved in my home? The pious words of the pastor did not console me, they infuriated me. I felt like punching him—and his God—in the gut.

These words of Job, pronounced devoutly by this pious preacher, only intensified the trauma of the occasion. That night, Saturday night, the members of my family stayed in the homes of neighbors devoid of any personal clothes to wear to church the next day. When we arrived at church, clumsily dressed in the odd clothes of neighborhood farmers, we were a little late and obliged to walk, quite embarrassed and anxious, to the very front row of the church.

When church was over, the preacher informed the congregation of our loss and again sought to console us with the assurance that God really loved farmers like us. The piety of the pastor and the community whose sympathy he sought to articulate became too much for me as the trauma intensified. I rose, said thanks, and announced that we had to leave.

We walked down the aisle even more embarrassed and anxious, the words of Job still ringing in my ears.

Over the years that followed, I made the book of Job the object of my personal research. I came to recognize that this book, in spite of my earliest memory of the so-called "patience of Job," was one of the great classical pieces of literature in the ancient Near East with precedents in several cultures other than ancient Israel.

In 1985 I published a major commentary on *The Book of Job* in *The Old Testament Library* series. In my Preface to that work I claim to have researched the most significant literary and theological works on the book of Job. I explored especially the language of the legal metaphor found throughout the book. I also examined the unique literary features of the book, demonstrating how the artistic and the theological are closely interwoven.

Subsequently, I wrote a range of papers on chapters and themes in the book of Job. One example, "Is the wild ox willing to serve you?," is located in volume three of *The Earth Bible Series* and explores the question of whether this passage (Job 39:9–12) challenges the mandate to dominate in Genesis 1:26–28.

My interest in Wisdom literature and ecological hermeneutics led me to reread the book of Job to ascertain whether Job's search for meaning is not ultimately a search for Wisdom in a world where justice seems to be lacking.

Accordingly, I titled the book *Finding Wisdom in Nature* with a subtitle specifying my approach, which I identify as *An Eco-Wisdom Reading of the Book of Job.* This volume is found in the *Earth Bible Commentary* series.

Now, more than seventy years after my first encounter with the words of Job, I realize that there are deep dimensions to the book of Job upon which I have often reflected but never published. Some of these reflections are included in a work I prepared to help chaplains and pastoral workers support religious people who had experienced trauma, distress, or spiritual abuse.

Often, in workshops on this subject, it was the chaplains themselves who articulated their trauma. One chaplain recounted the pain he still felt after having walked through dead bodies in the famous killing fields of Vietnam, "a pain," he said, "that persisted in his soul."

Now I am ready to reread Job as a profound articulation of the reality of trauma in human life and distraught communities, acutely aware of the Wisdom orientation of the Job narrative. With the words of Job again ringing in my ears, I will seek to retrieve the significance of Job's traumatic experiences and the unique Wisdom therapy that followed. My language, I hope, will be readable by interested parties in a range of disciplines, not just biblical scholars.

Just as significant is my discovery that the many expressions of
trauma that the narrator has formulated in the book of Job may be
more than a memory of trauma traditions and legends. The figure
of Job and his trauma experiences may preserve, by the mystery
of metaphor, trauma experiences of the religious world where the
narrator lived, experiences that are still relevant today.

Just as significant are my recent interpretations of the
Scriptures with First Nations Australia, in the process of which
I discovered the trauma of the colonial curse that many of them
experienced. At certain points in the analysis of Job in the contemporary world, I discover portraits of God that are not only frightening but also pungent portrayals that, if taken seriously, would
be traumatic even today.

TRAUMA AND WISDOM IN JOB

The initial goal of this volume is to experience the trauma of Job as a unique personal encounter with his God. His trauma is "God trauma," more than everyday human misery. To facilitate this experience empathetically, I have employed a trauma hermeneutic.

After experiencing the trauma and frustration of Job, the task is to explore Job's amazing encounter with the Wisdom Therapist and to experience a mode of Wisdom therapy that is unique and thought-provoking. Wisdom therapy enables Job to gain new levels of consciousness that we are challenged to experience.

I accept the definition of trauma articulated by scholars such as Irene Smith Landsman,

> *Trauma and loss are experiences that push us to our limits. By definition trauma overwhelms our usual abilities to cope and adjust, calling into question the basic assumptions that organise our experience of ourselves, our relationships, the world, and the human condition itself. The crisis of trauma is pervasive, altering emotional, cognitive and behavioural experience, and the subjective experience of trauma not infrequently includes a crisis of meaning at a deep level.* (2002, 13)

As this definition suggests, trauma is an experience that may be explored in a variety of disciplines including psychology, sociology, literary studies, and theology. Trauma may also involve a "crisis of meaning at a deep level," a truth that, I believe, is acutely apparent in the experiences of Job and the narrator's rendition of these experiences.

Another definition of trauma that I found helpful is that of Jennifer Baldwin:

> *The word 'Trauma' etymologically derives from the Greek meaning 'Wound.' Trauma at a fundamental level means wounding. Wounding can occur when a part of who we are is exiled from social structures (sexual orientation or institutional racism), family norms (expectations of achievement, appearance or performance), personal expectations (feelings of being 'not good/pretty/smart etc.'), or life experiences that fundamentally change our belief of who we are or how the world works. (24)*

The trauma of Job may readily be identified as the experience of being "exiled" from the domains cited in the quotation above. The language of wounding, however, is even more appropriate. Job is portrayed as being wounded by being isolated from his friends, torn by loss of personal expectations and battered by spiritual experiences that challenged his beliefs. Especially relevant is the fact that Job repeatedly accuses God of "wounding" him in body, mind, and spirit. I believe, therefore, it is appropriate to speak of "God wounding" or "God trauma," as the title of this volume indicates. Throughout the book of Job, the narrator portrays Job claiming to be "wounded" by God in more ways than one.

A psychological definition of trauma is damage to the psyche as a result of a distressing event or an overwhelming amount of stress that exceeds the ability of the individual to cope. In Job's case, he claims the stress that he experiences is also due to the persistent harassment by God.

* * *

Before exploring the context of a given chapter in part I, I will begin with a brief but pointed synopsis of the specific trauma that Job experiences or to which his friends respond. This preface serves not only to focus the attention of the reader on the trauma or therapy under consideration but also to highlight the fact that in the journey of Job, the trauma experiences of Job are not confined to the devastating loss he experiences in the Prologue.

The narrator of the book of Job captures a range of trauma experiences that reflect Job's sense of deep despair, bitterness of spirit, spiritual abuse, loss of hope, and being attacked by his God. The trauma experiences of Job, who struggles to find ways of coping, provide a brilliant portrayal of the worlds of trauma that humans may encounter. The book of Job is more than a classic piece of ancient literature; it is a masterful synthesis of traumatic experiences and potential modes of Wisdom therapy.

* * *

To appreciate the Wisdom worldview involved in the book of Job, we need to take into account the Wisdom culture of the narrator and the Wisdom perspective that the narrator incorporates into the events and dialogue of the narrative.

The diverse understandings of Wisdom reflected in the narrative include inherent divine Wisdom, accumulated human Wisdom, innate Wisdom in nature, acquired Wisdom and primordial Wisdom (cf. Prov 8:22). For a detailed analysis of the three innate dimensions of Wisdom in the cosmos and nature see *The Wisdom Trinity* (Habel 2021).

*   *   *

Is there a time and place that might be discernible as the traumatic location of the narrator of the book of Job? Is there a plausible traumatic event or series of events that moved the narrator to portray the agonies of Job in such a brilliant portrayal of God traumas? Or is Job but a classic literary rendition of an ancient legend from the ancient Near East?

Scholars interested in the function of trauma in the formation of biblical texts have argued that traumatic events are often suppressed in the memory and not readily articulated in narrative form.

The book of Job has traditionally been interpreted as an Israelite expression of an ancient legend, preserving a tradition that for generations innocent humans have been afflicted with misery, despair, and agony. Most scholars have not seriously explored the possibility that the voice of Job reflects the trauma of the narrator or the narrator's community in a particular event or time of history.

In her article "Whispered in the Sound of Silence," Elizabeth Boase explores the traumatic location when the book of Jonah was written, a traumatic location the details of which are "silent" in the book of Jonah. She writes,

> *The current reading assumes that the intended audience of the Book of Jonah lived in the region of Judah under Persian occupation. Locating the book within this period and setting provides an important clue to the rhetorical context into which the book enters. For this community, the events of*

the Babylonian destruction of Jerusalem and the subsequent
deportations were past events and construed as a watershed
in their life. (2017, 7)

In the light of parallel trauma readings of biblical texts, such
as Liz Boase's reading of Jonah cited above, I have now been challenged to attempt the almost impossible and identify a plausible
audience for the book of Job.

The insights of Tiffany Houck-Loomis provide a reasonable basis for locating the book of Job in the postexilic period.
She argues that Job is a "fictional character narrated within the
postexilic context of ancient Israel" (2015, 196). At this point I
would suggest that the narrator creates this "fictional character"
using well-known ancient Near Eastern legends about the innocent sufferer.

Houck-Loomis contends that the character of Job represents
a critique of the postexilic Deuteronomy covenant theology of
reward as a consequence of obedience to the Covenant God and
punishment as a result of disobedience to the covenant God, the
theology that Job's friends vigorously defend. Job's vehement
critique of this theology represents a community in tension with
the wider "faithful" Israelite covenant-oriented "community
unable and unwilling to deconstruct its deeply held image of God"
(Houck-Loomis, 2015, 195).

I would argue that the specific community in postexilic Israel
that the narrator of Job represents is a traumatized community
of the wise, adherents of a Wisdom School theology, a community I shall hereafter designate as the "Wisdom community." The
narrator belongs to the Wisdom School of thought, a feature that
is evident throughout the discourse, culminating first of all in the
Wisdom manifesto of chapter 28 and then in the Wisdom therapy
of chapters 38–39.

In my opinion, the narrator is clearly one of the wise and presumably represents a discrete Wisdom community that has experienced the destruction of Zion, the exile of the Israelite leaders, and the stress of postexilic life in Judah.

Another feature that I believe is relevant is that the narrator portrays Job, during his trauma discourses, as in relationship with El, El Shaddai, and El Eloah, not YHWH, the God of Israel. Nevertheless, it is YHWH, the God of Israel, who is portrayed as responsible for the family tragedy that Job experiences in the prologue narrative.

And so I ask, when would a community of Israel imagine itself in a world where El was their God, the God that Abraham knew when he first lived in the land of Canaan? That question leads me to suggest that the Wisdom community, represented by Job, experienced extreme trauma when they were abandoned by the God of Israel, when the divine presence (*kabod YHWH*) departed from Zion, leaving the land of Israel tantamount to the land of Canaan where Abraham settled.

In addition, many of the leaders of Israel, prophets, priests, and royal stock, were taken into captivity. Those left behind in Canaan were, among others, the farmers, laborers, and, it seems, members of a Wisdom community. Those who returned from exile were ardent adherents of the Mosaic covenant and the Covenant God.

This isolated Wisdom community may have responded, as does Job, with more than a sense of abandonment. They may well have believed that they were forced to live with a cruel God who treated them as guilty, the God of traditional covenant theology. And the three friends may well represent the prophets, fathers, and priests of Israel who also point the finger of guilt at those left behind.

And if the community left behind in Canaan is a traumatized community of the Wisdom School, they may then have returned to their roots to discern the God of Wisdom they once knew and explored the primordial for hope and healing rather than the traditions of Moses, Zion, and the Israelite covenant.

The vision of the basket of good and bad figs in Jeremiah 24 may well be relevant. The "good figs" are the leaders of Judah taken into exile—the king, the princes, the craftsmen, and the priests. YHWH promises to set his eyes on them for good, to bring them back to their land and give them a heart to know YHWH as God.

The "bad figs" are the remnant of the people left behind in Judah, a remnant that YHWH will make a horror, a taunt, and a curse, sending sword, famine, and pestilence until they are destroyed from the land given to their fathers.

With the message of Jeremiah still ringing in their ears, the community left behind would be coming to terms with the divine message that they are the bad figs about to be cursed, while those who returned from exile are the community blessed by YHWH. It is precisely a community of these "bad figs" that may be the community that the Wisdom narrator represents and portrays through the person of Job, who experiences the curse of the Covenant God.

In my trauma reading of the book of Job, I contend that while the narrator relates the experiences of an individual called Job, he is probably also representative of a specific postexilic Wisdom community that experienced collective trauma. In any case, the narrator is clearly a student of the ancient Wisdom School.

*   *   *

A crucial step in this hermeneutic is to identify with the party or parties experiencing the trauma under investigation. By so doing, the reader seeks to empathize with the person or community experiencing the trauma so as to understand the nature, force, and dimensions of the trauma and its potential healing. These dimensions may be emotional, communal, psychological, spiritual, or theological.

One of the ways to facilitate this empathy is to study the language employed, the expressions of angst, fear, desire, terror, and despair that the narrator, poet, or sage uses to describe the trauma being experienced. In this analysis, it is helpful to discern where and how the specific symptoms of trauma are reflected or hidden in the text.

The symptoms of psychological trauma that I found helpful in reading the text of Job afresh include shock and denial, anger and aggression, disturbed sleep, extreme anxiety, disassociation, and physical distress.

In my analysis of the book of Job that follows, I believe each of these symptoms of trauma are expressed by Job and captured at various points in the language of the Wisdom narrator.

Pivotal also for reading the book of Job is to recognize that Job, the individual experiencing the trauma, may represent both individuals and communities that experience extreme loss and pain. The Job of the legend is more than an isolated human from distant memory. Numerous communities in the past have experienced comparable crises and suffered extreme trauma. The trauma of Job is more than legend, even if we do not know precisely from when and where the narrator is reviving this memory.

The friends of Job, however, represent a different community. They seem to belong to an ancient Israelite tradition that views God as a righteous ruler who rewards good and punishes evil. They offer counsel for Job from within the parameters of their traditional beliefs about the Covenant God of Israel.

The wider context of the book of Job is the Wisdom School or tradition. Not only is Job introduced as one of the wise who "feared God and shunned evil," but both he and his friends reflect on how the Wisdom of their God is involved in the trauma crisis that Job has experienced.

Ultimately, however, the narrator takes us beyond the limited responses of the main protagonists of the legend and introduces a Wisdom therapy administered by a divine therapist whose presence and perspective represent a profound Wisdom worldview. A Wisdom therapy, I would argue, is reflected in the stages of Job's trauma journey in part II of this volume.

*   *   *

The function of the narrator in the design, wording, and focus of this text is more complex than I had ever imagined. The narrator of Job is much more than a "narrator" of an oral tradition or a literary artist. He is a creative historian, an empathetic member of a local postexilic community, an ardent Wisdom advocate, and a radical theologian.

Houck-Loomis speaks of Job as a "fictional character narrated within the postexilic context of ancient Israel" (2015, 196). I would modify this identification and explore how the narrator has taken a figure from an ancient legend and created a character that reflects the trauma of a historical situation. In contemporary terms, the text of the book of Job is an ancient form of *historical fiction*.

The author of this historical fiction narrative is more than a masterful literary artist. He belongs to a postexilic community that has experienced a range of traumatic experiences. The narrator does not merely report or describe what has happened and how his community has responded. Instead, he has a profound empathy for his community and is ready to portray its trauma in the most powerful personal terms through the character of Job. In contemporary terms, the narrator is *an empathetic interpreter* of the suppressed feelings of a traumatized community.

In the face of the dominant covenant theology of reward and retribution of the postexilic community, the narrator portrays the thinking of Job and his friends as expressions of the doubt and despair of his community about the acceptability of the God of the covenant tradition. In so doing, the narrator progressively undermines the value of trusting in the Covenant God. In contemporary terms, the Wisdom narrator is a *radical subversive theologian*.

The narrator, I would argue, belongs to the Wisdom School of thought and represents a Wisdom community surrounded by a postexilic covenant-oriented Israelite society. In addition to employing the character of Job to undermine the Covenant God tradition, the narrator has the courage to resurrect a suppressed tradition of the Wisdom God, the Primordial Scientist who discerns Wisdom as an innate cosmic force. He revives the belief of the Wisdom School that Wisdom is the relevant agency for healing the traumatized community to which he belongs. In contemporary terms, the narrator is a *Wisdom scientist with a cosmic consciousness*.

*   *   *

*More than 2000 years ago,
the narrator of the book of Job
related how Job
was challenged by
the Wisdom Therapist
to
take a radical leap of faith,
to dismiss mortal miseries
by searching cosmic mysteries,*

to expunge the terror of trauma
by celebrating the wonders of the wild,
and
to replace the celestial deity,
the righteous God of retribution,
with the Presence of Wisdom,
a therapeutic Mentor,
permeating the cosmos,
guiding him to find answers
to the Eternal Why
and
the Eternal Where:
"Where can Wisdom be found?"
Where?
Where this God,
the Wisdom Therapist,
read the landscape,
and invited Job
to do the same!

I

God Trauma
Job 1–27

PART I OF this trauma reading of the book of Job covers a wide range of episodes and experiences, from the cruel acts of God that initiate and intensify Job's trauma to the closing word of Job declaring an oath of integrity. While the contents of the trauma chapters in part I, reflected in the table of contents, focus on the specific traumas experienced by Job, it is helpful to highlight the range of traumatic experiences described in these chapters of the book of Job and the questions they raise about the traditional God that Job knew.

The trauma experiences embedded in episodes in this half of the book of Job include 1) the extreme pain experienced when there seems to be no reason to stay alive and when death at birth or even suicide is an inviting alternative, 2) the bitterness of experiencing the betrayal of friends who assume guilt as the reason for suffering and reject any appeal to accept the word of the sufferer, and 3) the frightening angst of the believer who has an acute sense that God relishes terrorizing them as if they were one of the wicked.

As Job's trauma intensifies, he experiences a loss of faith in the *imago Dei* tradition that promised humans a life as beings blessed with the image of God rather than the image of being a slave, the terrifying anguish of contemplating facing God in court when God is the fierce adversary rather than a fair judge, and the devastating feeling that the inherent Wisdom of God has been overwhelmed by his fierce, limitless power, leaving innocent victims in misery.

Job's bitter suffering in the soul brings nothing but nightmares when God seems to be a celestial spy rather than a compassionate companion, and a tragic loss of hope even when the innocent sufferer takes the bold step of confronting God with the truth.

CHAPTER 1

Family Tragedy and Denial

Job 1–2

> *The tragic loss*
> *of all an individual's*
> *possessions and family,*
> *or a community's meaningful world,*
> *under whatever disastrous circumstances,*
> *may cause the person*
> *or the community to experience*
> *a trauma*
> *that initially overwhelms*
> *their coping mechanisms.*

THE WIDER CONTEXT for the book of Job is the Wisdom School of the ancient world. The Wisdom School refers to the thinking, techniques, and traditions of a major body of the ancient Israelite community known as "the wise." The wise were a discrete part of that community, distinct from the priests, prophets, royalty, and other leading figures in that society. The narrator of Job, it would seem, is a representative of just such a Wisdom community.

There is evidence to suggest that in Egypt and Israel there were actual "schools" of wise men in locations like the royal court where they explored cosmic questions about how to live wisely and gave counsel to the leaders in society.

The Wisdom School refers to an orientation that involves learning via critical observation and rational analysis rather than revelation from a deity or a traditional message from religious leaders. This school of thought included close observation of both the natural world and human behavior. Wisdom thinking was akin to what we would call today "scientific analysis": the wise were the "scientists" of old, and the subject of their analysis was understood as both a mystery and a reality.

The full significance of this Wisdom orientation becomes apparent later in the book of Job when we meet God, the Wisdom Scientist, and when Job experiences Wisdom therapy. In the prologue, however, we are introduced to Job who "feared God and shunned evil," a traditional characteristic of the wise (cf. Job 28:28, Prov 3:7).

Job 1–2 is the prologue in which the narrator, clearly a member of the Wisdom School of thought, introduces a legendary portrayal of God and dubious beliefs about who will be exposed in the course of the volume. Job is one of the wise whose perspectives about life, Wisdom, God, and the cosmos will be explored and challenged.

In the prologue, Job, portrayed as a human being in crisis, is introduced as the human exemplar to be "observed" or "researched" by the empathetic reader who, as a result, has the potential to learn the ways of the School of the Wise.

Especially poignant for a Wisdom community is the image of a God who is portrayed as the source of unwarranted disasters, a God with whom they can no longer relate, a God who is boldly identified by the narrator as YHWH, the Covenant God of Israel.

The Character of Job

The opening scene for Job's traumatic experiences is the world of ancient legend. In that world, the narrator introduces Job as a paragon of piety and Wisdom, a colorful hero at the pinnacle of success, poised for a fall.

Four attributes characterize Job: he is described as "blameless and upright, who feared God and shunned evil" (Job 1.1). The term "blameless" (*tam*) defines Job as a person who has the utmost integrity, is free from sin, is right with God and is at peace with the world. Being "upright" (*yashar*), he is honest, truthful, and righteous. As one who fears God, Job is one of the wise who follows the path of Wisdom and goodwill. In line with these Wisdom attributes lies Job's total commitment to "shun evil" of any kind.

As a wise man who feared God and shunned evil, Job is apparently a symbol of the narrator's world, a local Wisdom community of ancient Israel.

Job has an ideal family and a wealth of material possessions. He is clearly portrayed as blessed in a way consistent with his piety. He is even described as "the greatest among the people of the East" (Job 1:3). To illustrate the integrity and piety of Job, the narrator recounts how Job acts as a mediator who atones for the sins that his children may have committed during their round of feasts. He then joins them in celebration, after their festivities, and sacrifices a burnt offering, declaring,

> *Perhaps my sons have sinned,*
> *and cursed God in their hearts.* (1:5)

The portrayal of Job's character presents the model of an ideal human being who would presumably have the Wisdom and the resilience of a community to help him withstand experiences that might well induce trauma of one kind or another.

The God of Unwarranted Disasters

The second scene in the prologue of the book of Job is the celestial assembly where the narrator introduces the dubious character of God. This God is identified as YHWH, the God of the

Israelites, a title never employed personally by Job during his poetic discourses.

In the celestial assembly, this God meets with the sons of God, the members of the celestial assembly, which includes a messenger called "the Satan," "the Advocate," or "the Accuser," who patrols Earth below.

In the course of the conversation, YHWH asks the Accuser,

> *Have you marked my servant, Job?*
> *Truly there is no one like him on earth,*
> *a blameless and upright man,*
> *who fears God and shuns evil.* (1:8)

God is portrayed as bragging to his assembly about Job, whom he views as one of a kind among mortals, an ideal wise human being. The Accuser then challenges God's bragging by asserting that Job only fears God because God has placed a hedge of blessings around him that have made him rich and famous. The Accuser then asserts that were God to stretch forth his hand and strike all Job's possessions he would "curse you to your face" (1:11).

The challenge of the Accuser provokes this God to justify his bold claim. God has no second thoughts. Job is immediately made the victim of this God's bias. The game is on! Who will win? Will Job curse God publicly if all his possessions are taken? Will he be traumatized and reject God? Or will he submit meekly?

By portraying God with this foolish mindset, the narrator sets the stage for a progression of oppressive images of God that follow in subsequent chapters.

Disasters that Cause Trauma

The hidden cause of potential trauma for Job is the result of the bargain made in heaven, the gamble of God to allow the Accuser to strike all of Job's possessions. Job is framed!

A series of unwarranted disasters are reported, the messenger in each case declaring that Job is the sole survivor.

> The first disaster spells the end of Job's agricultural world. His animals are all captured and all the "boys" working in the field are murdered.
>
> In the second disaster, the "fire of God" destroys all of Job's pastoral pursuits, killing all the animals and murdering the shepherd "boys" attending them.
>
> The third disaster marks the end of Job's trading activities. His camels are all captured and his caravan "boys" are also murdered.
>
> The final disaster is even more personal and horrendous. A great wind comes from the desert, destroys Job's home, and murders all his children.

These four disasters, each of which involves killing, would appear to be enough to provoke the anger or angst of any mortal, including Job. Not only does Job lose all his possessions, but all of his work "boys" and all of his family "boys" are murdered. He is faced with death and utter darkness.

A Personal Disaster

When God's celestial assembly meets again, God begins by bragging that he has won the wager. Job remains blameless and upright, despite the fact that the Accuser "incited me against him to swallow him, all for nothing" (2:3).

Now this God, ignoring his earlier bias, is ready to blame the Accuser for inciting God to "swallow" Job with disasters. For the Accuser, however, the game is not over. He makes the claim that it is one thing to destroy all of one's possessions, it is quite another to make life miserable by filling the human body with pain and pus.

The Accuser again challenges God and claims that Job, afflicted with pain, would curse God to his face. Once again God does not waver but permits the Accuser to proceed. God declares, "So be it! He is in your hands, only watch over his life" (2:6).

Job may also be traumatized when he is afflicted with foul sores from the soles of his feet to the crown of his head. Job's life has become the epitome of misery. His potential trauma is tantamount to hell on Earth.

Trauma Denial

At this point most interpreters have assumed that the narrator's presentation of Job's response to the disasters he experiences is a pious acceptance of what happened. Despite everything that happened, "Job does not sin with his lips" (2:10). Job's actions may be an ironic portrayal of a wider Israelite community that piously accepts its fate as the will of their Covenant God.

A closer reading, however, reveals that Job's response is a form of pious denial. He refuses to admit that the pain, the disasters, and the murders he is facing are due to the cruel hand of a biased deity. He is denying that he is faced with a trauma arising from the reality of the crisis he has endured.

Denial is recognized as a psychological defense against trauma, a mechanism that disavows the harsh realities of the situation. I believe there are three ways in which Job expressed denial in the face of the trauma he would naturally experience when confronted by such cruel disasters.

a. The Naked Truth

After the first series of disasters, the narrator reports that Job arose, tore his robe, cut off his hair, and fell on the ground. These reactions would suggest that Job may be in the initial stages of a brutal trauma. The narrator, however, adds that Job also worshipped and uttered his famous cry of acceptance, a cry I would suggest, is tantamount to a denial of trauma:

> *Naked I came from my mother's womb,*
> *and naked I shall return there.*
> *YHWH gives and YHWH takes away.*
> *Blessed be the name of YHWH.* (1:21)

Job's denial is presented as a pious expression of worship, a spiritual avoidance of the brutality of the moment, perhaps also a reflection of a faithful community coming to terms with a disaster such as the Fall of Jerusalem.

Job first declares that he was naked, devoid of possessions when he was born and that he will be without possessions once he dies. His declaration is a denial of the fact that between life and death he has been dispossessed, crushed, and humiliated. He then affirms the sovereign power of YHWH to give or take as a reality he must recognize regardless of his faithful relationship with his God. He surrenders all his rights to YHWH and denies his own life story. In so doing, he denies his trauma.

b. An Honest Wife

After his second cruel experience, Job again reacts in a way that would suggest he was traumatized. He takes a potsherd, scratches the boils across his body, and sits in a pile of ashes. At that point his wife, obviously angry and distraught, screams:

> *You still hold fast to your integrity?*
> *Curse God and die!* (2:9)

Job's wife, who offers no traditional form of comfort, is perhaps advocating a form of suicide to resolve the situation. In her mind, if Job curses God, he would be struck dead on the spot. And the contemplation of suicide is itself a form of trauma that is a real option, an option Job explores in chapter 3. At this point, however, Job's denial persists. He responds to his wife by declaring,

> *You talk like a shameless fool!*
> *Shall we accept only good from God*
> *and not accept evil?* (2:10)

The "evil" (*ra'*) that Job experiences refers, at first glance, to the calamities he has experienced. Yet there is a subtle hint that God is the source of other forms of evil, a traumatic option that Job cannot quite deny.

Job, in his anguish, has become egocentric. He is concerned only about his own pain, his own loss, his own relationship with God. He seems to forget his family and shows no compassion for his wife who has also lost her family. Job's wife, however, has pointed to the crux of the crisis—the truth that the traditional teaching of divine retribution has been exposed as invalid, a truth Job has yet to explore.

c. Silent Anguish

After his harsh encounter with his wife, Job joins the friends who come to console and comfort him. Job's condition was such that his friends hardly recognize him. In response, they wail and fling dust into the air, ostensible expressions of empathy. They then sit on the ground in silence for seven days and seven nights.

I would suggest that Job's silence is another expression of denial. He does not share his story or his feelings with his wife or his friends. He sits in silent denial on the ground.

The reality that Job was not calm and composed, happily blessing God for all the "good and evil" he had experienced, is evident from the closing comment of the narrator:

> *No one spoke a word to him,*
> *for they saw that his anguish was very great.* (2:13)

Seven days may be seen as a symbol of complete acceptance of the situation, but as the following chapter reveals, these seven days allow time for the bitterness and rage of Job's initial trauma to build.

Subversive Caricature

Given that most interpreters view the portrait of God in the prologue as a fragment of ancient mythic thinking, the confronting portrait of YHWH as the subversive source of trauma is largely ignored. The narrator, however, confronts us with an image of a God that is not only a caricature of true divinity but also an irresponsible lord of a heavenly council that is ready to play ugly games with humankind.

The implication of this portrayal is that YHWH is here depicted as a subversive God who creates trauma, not as a compassionate creator and a guarantor of justice. If I were to live in a world with such a devious deity as a living reality, I would be devastated. To confront this God of unwarranted disasters may well provoke trauma in the believer—God trauma.

Such a blatant portrayal of God as a celestial being without scruples may also be a way of the narrator raising the question of whether the community whom Job represents ultimately discovers another divine reality in another dimension of the universe, a dimension known as Cosmic Wisdom.

It is time to dismiss YHWH as the God presented in the prologue of Job and follow the trail of Job to explore subsequent images of God and the existential questions raised by the God trauma experienced by Job and the community he may represent. The ultimate goal is to discern a deeper dimension of spiritual reality, the Wisdom *innate* in the depths of the cosmos.

A second implication of this trauma reading is that it exposes the falsity of the popular image of Job as the symbol of patience and piety. Job's pious responses are not expressions of patience and devotion but of trauma denial. It is precisely this danger—hiding trauma beneath pious consolation—that a trauma reading exposes.

CHAPTER 2

Meaningless Existence

Job 3

In the context of deep despair,
isolation, broken relationships
and shattered dreams,
a person or community may experience
the trauma of meaningless existence.
Such a person or community
may scream the eternal why:
Why was I born if there is no meaning in life?
With no reason to live,
that person may also contemplate suicide,
escaping to the land of the dead,
a world at peace.

THE LITERARY CONTEXT of Job's violent outburst in chapter 3 is the horrendous series of unwarranted disasters and the personal bodily misery that Job has experienced at the hands of his God recorded in chapters 1–2. Associated with these disasters is Job's trauma denial, his pious expressions of faith in a God who can crush humans with "evil" acts from on high.

For seven days, Job remains silent with no comfort or consolation from his friends. For seven days, Job is undergoing an inner upheaval that explodes in chapter 3. The literary context also raises the question of contemplating suicide as an answer to the cruelty of the moment. Job's wife has recommended a form of euthanasia: "curse God and die." Job, it seems, does not actually plan to commit suicide, but he contemplates death and the land of the dead as the land of desirable dreams.

A close reading of Job's discourse reveals, I believe, evidence that Job represents a Wisdom community that has experienced extreme traumatic events. Verse 22 clearly reflects the mindset of the Wisdom School. Job claims that his *derek* has been hedged in by Eloah, preventing him from finding meaning in life. The term *derek* is a technical term of the Wisdom School referring to the innate Wisdom, character, and purpose of an individual (Habel 2015, ch. 2).

The Trauma of Being Born

The narrator portrays Job beginning his outcry of agony by cursing the day of his birth, by seeking to make that day a day of darkness and trauma. Job's opening words are a threefold, "Damn, damn, damn!"

The dimensions of Job's initial trauma are evident in the blatant brutality of the language of his curse. Both day and night are cursed because they both played a role in his birth.

In verses 4–5, there are six incantations summoning darkness and oblivion on the day of Job's birth. Not only is light to be terminated, the shadow of death is also summoned to destroy Job's birthday. Finally, Job even calls upon the demons of the day to play their evil role and end the day of his birth. Job has pronounced incantations designed to transform his day of birth from one of blessing and joy into one of trauma and curse.

In verses 6–9, we hear nine incantations relating to the night of Job's birth. In verse 6, we hear three incantations summoning darkness and oblivion. In verse 7, we hear three incantations summoning barrenness and chaos. In verse 8, we hear three more incantations summoning darkness and oblivion. Job yearns for the night of his birth to be obliterated.

Why? In verse 10, the rationale for these ugly curses is made explicit. Because the womb of Job's mother was not closed permanently so that Job could not be born.

Why? Because of the misery, the trauma of being born, that Job is now experiencing. Because the Wisdom community, whom Job represents, is forced to live in isolated despair with no apparent hope in the future.

In the design of the book of Job, Job's words are not only the ugly moaning and screaming of a person in pain. These curses are basic to the plot of the book that follows. Job has not only called for his origins to be negated, but he also invokes forces of darkness and sets himself against God. Job may not have cursed God to his face, but he has damned the very birth that his God facilitated. The question remains whether Job's curses will, in fact, provoke divine action and terminate Job's trauma or Job's life.

This portrayal of total despair probably reflects the trauma of the Wisdom community whom Job represents and whose angst the narrator articulates as Job's inner anguish. In that traumatic context, those who view themselves as the victims of abandonment after events like the Fall of Jerusalem are initially ready to invoke forces of darkness in the face of despair.

Contemplating the Pleasure of Death

In the second stanza of this chapter (vv. 11–19), the focus moves from birth to death, from curse to lament. Job asks *why, why, why?* The Wisdom community asks *why, why, why?*

Job's initial *why* relates to why he did not die at birth. Being a stillborn baby would not eventuate in a life of trouble and trauma. Having died at birth would mean that Job is lying in repose, at peace in the land of the dead. If he were a "hidden still birth," an aborted fetus, he would never have experienced the cruel light of day and all the pain that comes with living.

The language of Job's lament reveals a latent desire to end his life, the possibility of death, the trauma of contemplating suicide. Euthanasia is appealing at this point. This option is also reflected in Job's vivid portrayal of the land of the dead as a realm of peace, of freedom from oppression and ultimately from God, the celestial taskmaster.

A significant feature of these laments is an intricate pattern of reversals: from birth to prebirth, from light to darkness, from present-day trauma to the pleasure of life in the underworld, from turmoil on Earth to peace in Sheol.

The trauma of Job at this point is the contemplation of a better life in the land of the dead, the trauma of contemplating death. All are equal in the land of the dead, liberated from the oppression experienced on Earth. Life is depicted as a form of harsh slavery and enforced labor (cf. 7:1–2); only death can liberate the living. For Job, at this point in his trauma journey, death is a genuine option, a deep desire, an inviting possibility.

Life in the land of the dead is preferable to the misery of isolation for the surviving Wisdom community, wherever they are located.

Contemplating the Eternal Why

Job's death wish persists in the closing stanza of this poem (vv. 20–26). His cries of "why" continue as he explores the misery of meaningless existence. To be "bitter in spirit" is to know the trauma of inner pain in the face of a cruel world surrounding the sufferer. Job again contemplates the land of the dead as a desirable domain, a world of "treasures" for a person whose life is hell (3:21). The grave is an anticipated place of delight and joy in contrast to a life of trauma.

The profound core of this lament is in verse 23. Job asks why life is given,

> To a person whose way (derek) is hid,
> hedged around by Eloah?

Pivotal to an appreciation of this cry are two dimensions captured in the language the narrator employs for Job to articulate the trauma of "meaningless existence."

The first dimension is the expression "hedged." The *hedge* is a symbol of the forces or factors that surround and suffocate the person in the throes of trauma. The hedge blocks the pathway to find meaning in life. Ironically, the Accuser had accused God of surrounding Job with a "hedge" of blessings, a hedge that provided only the joys and delights of life with a generous God.

For Job and the Wisdom community that Job represents, the hedge is the opposite—a boundary of inescapable misery created by God, here identified as the ancient Eloah.

Crucial in this context is that which is hidden by the hedge, namely the "way." The English translation does not capture the depth of meaning involved when the Wisdom term *derek* (way) is used. Elsewhere I have defined *derek* as

> The "way" of something reflects its essential character, its internal impulse, its innate wisdom, whether it be the "way" of an eagle in the sky or the "way" of a snake on a rock. (Prov 30:19; 2014, 12)

Job is screaming because his very being, his meaning in life, his inner self, is hidden by the hedge of horrors that surround him. With this outburst, Job begins to confront God with the pain of trauma—his meaningless existence.

A crucial dimension of that trauma is elaborated further in his final scream (vv. 25–26). Job knows only a life of turmoil with no rest, no peace, no future. The contemplation of suicide still hovers in the background. The land of the dead is still the only place where Job can imagine peace. The *derek*, the innate Wisdom that inspires meaning, has been hidden by a cruel God.

In his article on trauma involving "Reading Job with People Living with HIV," Gerald West recounts how one of his listeners responds to the text of Job 3, which reinvokes the trauma he has experienced living with HIV:

> *As we explored Job 3 together in that formative Contextual Bible Study, a young man . . . voiced his despair, declaring that he knew how Job felt fantasizing about his death. Trembling with emotion he told us how he had to fight the desire to take his own life after he was diagnosed as HIV-positive.* (2016, 213)

While Job, or the young man whose feelings were expressed above, may not have chosen to commit suicide, stage one in Job's journey was to let the emotions associated with his trauma be expressed . . . boldly. Job was, for this youth, "an ancestor in the faith who refused to be silent" (West 222).

A crucial insight that emerges from an empathy analysis of Job chapter 3 is the value of screaming *the eternal Why* in the face of grievous personal pain and meaningless disaster. The *the eternal Why* that Job evokes in the midst of his screaming is a question posed by thinkers and theologians for hundreds of years.

In the case of Job, and people in extreme trauma, this question is not only existential but also cruel and debilitating. This question may even rouse the frightening question of whether suicide is the answer. Job's cry is a plausible precedent for those who experience the trauma of meaningless existence to scream *the eternal Why*.

CHAPTER 3

Counsel of Eliphaz

Job 4–5

*Trauma counseling is nothing new
and the citation of so-called
spiritual revelations
to counsel
and calm the traumatized
person or community
may well be evaluated
as spiritual abuse
by sufferers who know
the depths of despair.*

ELIPHAZ IS THE first of Job's counselors and would-be therapists to respond to Job's initial outburst. He breaks the sympathetic silence of the three friends with the affirming tone of an ancient counselor who assumes a common tradition on which a word of Wisdom may be based.

He does not, however, link his response to any of the disasters Job has experienced or to the specifics of Job's trauma of contemplating death. Instead, he claims to have had a weird "charismatic" revelation about the nature of the human condition and can verify his teaching from personal experience and observation. As such, he represents the prophetic tradition that maintains its own revelation of truth.

In the light of his revelation and experience, Eliphaz recommends that Job repent, plead with El for mercy, and accept his plight as due divine discipline.

In subsequent speeches (chapters 15 and 22), Eliphaz is much more aggressive and accuses Job of subverting the fear of God and refusing to heed the advice of wise elders. Eliphaz again repeats the gist of his revelation from the Spirit and declares,

> *What are mortals that they should be pure,*
> *those born of a woman that they should be in the*
>   *right?* (15:14)

Like his friends, Eliphaz seems to revel in extensive portrayals of the wicked and their ultimate fate, a portrayal of prophetic judgment that is presumably designed to awaken Job and facilitate repentance.

The narrator may be living in a community that is subservient to what I have designated the Covenant God, the God who rewards or punishes in accordance with his people's obedience to the covenant. The background to this Covenant God is clearly articulated by Houck-Loumis who writes,

> *In the light of the Deuteronomistic theology (reward as a*
> *consequence of obedience to the covenant and, conversely,*
> *punishment for disobedience) across the Hebrew Bible, and*
> *in particular in the first and second cycles of Job (Job 1.5;*
> *1.22; 4.69; 5.25; 8.4; 11.6b; 11.13–20; 18.5–21; 20),*
> *the character of Job may be read as a subversive critique.*
> (2015, 195)

The community that Job represents has clearly been part of a people for whom the covenant and the Covenant God was once fundamental to their worldview. The friends are portrayed by the narrator as faithful adherents of the Covenant God. As Houck-Loumis states,

Job's friends are adamant that the circumstances that befell Job must be interpreted as punishment for wrongdoing per the Deuteronomistic covenant, the covenant ideology adopted within post-exilic Israel to ensure God's control over the events of the exile and God's promise of restoration based on Israel's renewed obedience. (2015, 195)

The covenant ideology of the community whom Eliphaz represents is apparent in chapter 22 where Eliphaz counsels Job to make a covenant and repent:

> *Come to terms with him and make a covenant.*
> *Your gain will be the Good One.*
> *Receive instruction from his mouth,*
> *and take his words to your heart.*
> *If you return to Shaddai you will be rehabilitated.*
> (22:21–23)

Eliphaz assumes that this Covenant God could rescue Job from his trauma if he submitted his case to that God with due contrition. With that God,

> *The poor have hope*
> *and deceit shuts her mouth.*
> *Blessed be the mortal whom God corrects.*
> *So do not reject the discipline of Shaddai.* (5:16–17)

Throughout his speeches, Eliphaz in no way considers the possibility that Job might be an innocent victim who is suffering unwarranted trauma. Eliphaz assumes Job is guilty, by virtue of his nature as an impure human, by virtue of sins he must have committed, and by virtue of his "obvious" depravity.

As a representative of the prophetic tradition of postexilic Israel, Eliphaz's counsel is tantamount to a harsh message of judgment, a message that the distraught Wisdom community in Canaan would find abusive rather than therapeutic. The voice of Eliphaz as a prophet may well recall the vision of Jeremiah that portrayed the communities left behind when the leaders of Judah went into exile as nothing but "bad figs" destined to be cursed (cf. Jer 24) and experience the trauma of divine rejection.

Declaring the Obvious

Eliphaz begins by declaring that he cannot resist responding to Job's situation. It's obvious! Surely a man with his history and his faith in the Covenant God must know the obvious:

What innocent person ever perished? (4:7)

According to Eliphaz, Job should know only too well that those who sow trouble reap it and that even lions know the truth. They too must perish! That teaching is presumed to be part of their common religious tradition, especially in the ancient Near East and the covenant community of Israel (e.g., Ps 37).

Eliphaz is aware that Job has himself been a counselor for those who are suffering and weak. In the eyes of Eliphaz, that means Job should appreciate the ultimate truth that the innocent do not perish, even if they suffer.

The Charismatic Moment

Eliphaz claims to have had a traumatic experience deep in the darkness of night. Like a prophet faced with the power of God's word, Eliphaz is faced with a spiritual terror.

> *A word came to me in stealth,*
> *my ear caught a sound of it*
> *in the trauma of night visions,*
> *in the slumber that falls heavy on humans.*
> *Terror faced me and shuddering!*
> *It left all my limbs trembling with fear.* (4:12–14)

Unlike Job's experiences of death and disaster, Eliphaz claims to have had a traumatic revelatory experience of a fearful unknown, a terror emanating from another realm. He recognizes, however, that his terror is in fact a mysterious wind/spirit (*ruach*) that makes him quiver with fear in anticipation of its ominous message. Ironically, the "wind/whirlwind" that Eliphaz experiences conveys a radically different message to that of the "whirlwind" Job later encounters as the divine Wisdom therapist, and the "terror" Job knows (3:25) as a debilitating force rather than an agent of revelation.

The narrator, writing from a Wisdom School perspective, by placing this alleged revelation in the speech of Eliphaz, seems to be implying that this "word" communicated from another realm is akin to the call experiences of prophets, and not as trustworthy as the experiences of the wise who "observed" the truth as ancient scientists.

The Ominous Message

The message Eliphaz receives from the mysterious spirit is blunt and brutal. Human beings are made of clay and therefore impure!

> *Can mortals be righteous before God?*
> *Humans pure before their Maker?*

Even angels are not pure before God. In short, this mysterious voice ostensibly proclaims the truth of what was later designated

by theologians as "original sin." The implication is that Job is clay
and therefore corrupt from the time of his birth and cannot ever
be free from sin.

In other words, Job is not only stricken with the trauma of
disasters and a meaningless existence, he is also expected to live
with the additional burden of original sin. The counsel of his charismatic friend only adds to his trauma; according to Eliphaz, Job
is born a sinner who will inevitably experience retribution.

Significantly, Job too explores human nature as he experiences
it through his trauma (chapter 7). His perspective, however, is
radically different. Instead of being born a human destined to sin
and suffer, he believes he is born a slave of God, born to experience
servitude and cruel oppression.

Later, in line with the ominous message from the wind/spirit,
Eliphaz adds,

> *Evil springs from the ground*
> *and trouble sprouts from the dry ground.*
> *A human is born for trouble*
> *as the sons of Reshef fly upward.* (5:6–7)

Eliphaz seems to go so far as to say that the ground (*'adama*)
from which Adam was formed is itself the source of evil. Earth is
then the source of original sin and human suffering. Humans live
amid the evils of Earth, including the sons of Reshef, the traditional source of pestilence and plagues.

Eliphaz is also claiming that the fate of God's people is not
confined to their breach of the covenant but is part of their destiny
as sinful humans, a doctrine that is completely at odds with the
beliefs of the Wisdom community. Yet Eliphaz confronts Job with
a closing message that sinful humans ultimately die "devoid of
Wisdom." The God of Eliphaz is the God of original sin, creating
humans from the corrupt clay of Earth and destined to be sinners.

CHAPTER 4

Suffocating Friends

Job 6

> *A person or community*
> *experiencing a cruel trauma*
> *that provokes the sufferer*
> *to contemplate suicide may*
> *experience additional trauma*
> *at the hands of*
> *counselors and would-be therapists*
> *who virtually suffocate their patient*
> *with pious platitudes*
> *and rough theological truths*
> *that cause a trauma of spiritual abuse.*

IN THIS DISCOURSE, Job responds to the ostensible empathy and pious theology of Eliphaz about original sin and divine discipline (in chapters 4 and 5). Job does not enter a debate about the theological stance taken by Eliphaz, the first of his friends. Instead, Job reiterates his earlier death wish and exposes the way his friends have treated him, suffocating him with their piety and devious doctrine. They are barren sources of comfort.

A suffering Wisdom community in postexilic Israel may well be surrounded by religious leaders and would-be friends from different traditions who seek to counsel the community Job represents with their understanding of God's message for the traumatized sufferer.

The narrator captures, via the portrayal of Job, just how devoid of empathy and understanding the advice of would-be therapists can be. The Covenant God of the postexilic community is no longer the God whom Job, as the spokesman for the Wisdom community, finds believable. And the surrounding community of Israel becomes a colony of false friends.

In his article on Job chapters 6 and 7, Houck-Loumis argues quite convincingly that the background to the book of Job is the Deuteronomistic covenant theology of reward and retribution.

> *Readers of this story today witness within the narrative a community unable and unwilling to deconstruct its deeply held image of God.* (Houck-Loomis, 2015, 195)

I would argue further that Job may represent a postexilic Wisdom community struggling with its experiences of this God in the context of the wider Israelite community of Israel that refuses to modify its faith in its Covenant God in the light of its exilic experiences. How does a community of "bad figs" come to terms with a Covenant God who has rejected them?

The Terrors of Eloah

Job begins his second cry of anguish and explains why his words of exclamation are so wild:

> *For the arrows of Shaddai are in me.*
> *My spirit imbibes their poison.*
> *The terrors of Eloah are arrayed against me.* (6:3)

Job has moved his focus from contemplating the inviting world of death to a direct accusation against his God. His trauma, he claims, is caused by the poisonous arrows of Shaddai, the celestial archer. Job frequently uses the verb "terrify" (*b't*), but the noun for *terrors* is found only here and in Psalm 88:16, a noun that is virtually equivalent in meaning to "trauma." Job is living in terror, a trauma he now claims is caused by a cruel heavenly hunter.

The image here is that of a helpless victim on Earth being bombarded by arrows dipped in poison to heighten the pain and the terror. Later, Bildad describes God as "the King of Terrors" (18:17), a portrait that highlights the celestial source of Job's trauma. There seems to be no escape for the victim of this scenario.

In spite of the cruelty Job believes he experiences at the hands of this God, this is the first point at which Job confronts God directly with the reality of Job's pain. Job may be suffering, but he will not let God off the hook! God must suffer too if God has any empathy for his victim.

The Comfort of Death

Job reiterates his longing for death but confronts his God with the angst of it all. If God keeps terrorizing Job with poisonous arrows, why does God not finish the job and kill Job? That would mean comfort! Then Job would revel in his demise. Unless, of course, God is enjoying the game of hunting Job and apparently this God must keep Job suffering.

Job complains that he has no hope for the future, no strength to keep going, no chance of success. Death is his only real comfort. But God denies him even that option.

False Friends

The heart of this outburst in chapter 6 is Job's portrayal of his fickle companions, so-called friends who only intensify his trauma rather than consoling him. The most powerful punch is found in his bold outcry:

> *The despairing need the loyalty of a friend*
> *when they forsake the fear of Shaddai.* (6:14)

When a person experiences deep trauma, a trauma that leaves the person bereft of faith in God, that moment is the time when a person needs a true friend. A genuine friend is needed when there is no sustenance from God, when the victim has forsaken the "fear of Shaddai." A true friend is a last resort. As Houck-Loomis states, *Job essentially tells his friends that just because their friend abandons God, they should not abandon him* (2015, 200).

According to Job, a despairing person needs "loyalty" (*chesed*) in times of crisis. *Chesed* involves an inner rapport of deep concern that outlasts breaches of faith. *Chesed* is the underlying loyalty that guarantees covenant relationships (II Sam 2:5–6; Ps 106:43–45). True loyalty is expected of a friend when all other support systems fail, including faith in God.

Job's friends, whom he here calls brothers, are like a fickle wadi, a stream that runs dry, a waterhole that disappears, a watercourse that twists and turns and fades away.

People is caravans and travelers on the road hope to find water to sustain them, but they only find dry creek beds. Or in the words of Job, his friends are like dry wadis; they cannot be trusted.

After his portrayal of false friends in general, Job addresses his three personal friends and challenges them to remember their past relationship with Job. He poses a series of questions about how he has treated them and now wants to know why his honest words about his trauma distress them and leave them unable to provide genuine support. They may have their say to correct Job, but they ignore his outcries.

> *Do you devise arguments to correct me,*
> *but count as wind the words of a despairing person?*
> (6:26)

Job screams at his friends with a final outcry:

> *Relent! Away with deceit.*
> *Relent! I am still in the right!* (6:29)

Job finds no comfort in the words of his friends, no consolation, no understanding. Job is alone without friends or God! He is smothered by loneliness and suffocating with despair.

A crucial insight, related to the experience of a suffering Wisdom community, is encapsulated in the line, "when they forsake the fear of Shaddai" (v. 14). *Fear* is a term derived from the Wisdom tradition that indicates both the expectation of insight and guidance from God. The assumption here is that a given community has reached the point where it has forsaken belief in its traditional deity and can discern no guidance.

In this chapter, however, we are also confronted with a bold portrayal of the loyalty of a true friend, unlike the friends who sought to comfort Job. Friendship here involves standing by, supporting and remaining loyal, regardless of the circumstances, even loss of faith or hope in God. In a true friendship relationship, God is secondary, a subject I explored many years ago in an article entitled, "Only the Jackal is my Friend" (Habel 1977).

CHAPTER 5

Human Oppression

Job 7

> *The person who has experienced*
> *the trauma of meaningless existence*
> *and the spiritual abuse*
> *of counselors*
> *about the nature of the human condition,*
> *may, upon painful reflection,*
> *experience the trauma of*
> *merciless human oppression,*
> *the bitterness of a soul*
> *provoked by*
> *nightmares about what it means*
> *to be a humiliated human.*

IN THE SEVENTH chapter of Job, we are confronted by a profound portrayal of a trauma experience, a portrayal that yields significant insights into our understanding of the nature of trauma and human loss.

The narrator portrays Job reflecting on the agony he has come to discern on being a human being. The disasters and losses outlined in the prologue are not the focus of Job's outburst in this chapter.

The trauma of contemplating death portrayed in chapter 3 lies in the background as Job considers escaping from the celestial Seeing Eye and residing in Sheol. In chapter 6, Job repeats his wish that he could be dead and cannot understand why God does not end his life.

The heartless counsel offered by Eliphaz is ignored and his claim that humans can never be pure before their Maker is countered by Job's bold declaration that humans can never be free and happy in this life.

The narrator in this discourse shows, through the agony of Job, how a human being experiencing extreme trauma can come to the frightening conclusion that misery, servitude, and suffering are inevitable consequences of being a human being living on Earth. He even goes so far as to laugh at the tradition that human beings are created in the image of God. They are not created to rule on Earth but to be slaves and hirelings.

Interpreters may read this as an ancient literary discourse by insightful authors about human nature and the difficult dimensions of being a human being. From a trauma perspective, however, this text goes beyond a literary discourse to being a bold revelation of the anguish and agony of individuals and communities that encounter a world where they experience the cruel intervention of unwarranted pain and loss. That experience challenges us to understand anew what it means to be a human being in a world of disasters.

In chapter 7, according to Houck-Loomis, "Job begins to challenge the ruling pedagogy of the entrenched God image at work within the community" (2015, 200). She argues quite plausibly,

I will show how these two speeches (Job 6–7) highlight the theological and psychological tensions potentially at stake within the post-exilic community of Israel, likely responsible for constructing this text. (2015, 196)

The wider community involved, as I now read the narrator's portrayal of Job, probably includes the "faithful" Israelite community, perhaps even postexilic, who refuses to modify its entrenched God image. The suffering Wisdom community is struggling to come to terms with the unwarranted disasters it has suffered at the hands of the Covenant God they knew and the radical Wisdom narrator who is exploring traditional images of God through the trauma journey of Job.

Through the trauma experience of Job, the traumatized Wisdom community is enabled, via the narrator, to encounter diverse images of God with the option of a Wisdom-inspired resolution.

A Trauma Reading of the Human Condition

Job begins by declaring that being a human being in his condition is a form of heartless slavery. He portrays his experience of being human in terms that are in direct contradiction to those of the *imago Dei* in Genesis 1 (Gen. 1:26–28), a dilemma explored later in this discourse. For Job, life as a human being is experienced as sheer servitude, devoid of hope. Severe trauma in the experience of Job is portrayed as a lifetime of endless slavery, not of dominion and power.

Another dimension of Job's misery is dark oppressive nights, inescapable nightmares that leave the sufferer screaming. The language describing Job's sleepless nights of endless agony suggests deep depression and despair.

Job's misery also extends to his body, which he describes as clad in worms and dust with a skin that "dries hard and suppurates." Persistent nightmares and ongoing physical pains are also recognized symptoms of psychological trauma. Job is both emotionally and physically in agony without any hope of relief, day or night.

A pivotal image is the expectation that his days end "when the thread runs out." The term *tiqwa* in its concrete sense is a thread or cord (as in Josh 2:18). Its abstract meaning is "hope," a central theme in the poetry of Job (4:6; 6:8; 14:7). Given the double entendre here, the sense seems to be that humans cling to an elusive thread as their last hope, but with death comes the termination of life and the slender thread of hope.

A realization by Job that human life, no matter how miserable, will come to an end provokes Job to taunt God with a bold satirical cry. The assumption of this sufferer is that God is like a celestial spy who enjoys watching humans like Job go through agony as a slave. Job taunts God with a declaration that he will eventually escape the Seeing Eye, the God who relishes watching humans like Job suffer.

Job describes God as a Seeing Eye who will one day be watching the show down on Earth called "Job" and discover he is not there. The show is over; the performer has not arrived. The day of Job's death provides a hint of comfort—escape from the eye of the celestial overlord.

In the midst of his endless pain, Job again reflects on the pleasure of death, of a peaceful life in the underworld of Sheol. The trauma of potential death experienced earlier in chapter 3 lies in the background.

The Spiritual Torment of the Soul

Job then declares he is ready to announce the truth of his situation. He reveals that his condition is more than one of physical pain or emotional misery. His trauma is spiritual and psychological. His "spirit" is tormented, and his "soul" knows sheer bitterness. He experiences his trauma as the result of spiritual abuse from a cruel God who controls Job as if he were a chaos deity, like the mythical Canaanite God, Yam.

Also significant is the fact that Job again complains bitterly about his dark experiences at night, his terrifying dreams and his unwanted visions. Dark nightmares of this nature are common among people who know extreme trauma and deep depression, whether emotional, spiritual, or social.

Job closes the second stanza of this chapter by again admitting his desire to die and escape what he calls living with the "strangling" of God. Death is better than a life of torture. In this terrifying condition it is understandable, therefore, that Job again taunts God with his assertion that he does not want life on Earth to last forever, given the misery it brings.

Dismissal of the *Imago Dei* Tradition

In the final stanza, Job is portrayed as making a parody of the hymnic version of the *imago Dei* found in Psalm 8:

> *What is man that you should remember him,*
> *mortal man that you should visit (pqd) him?*
> *You made him a little less than a god,*
> *crowning him with honour and glory.*
>   (Ps 8:5–6 NEB)

To appreciate the parody of this text in Job, we need to recognize key terms employed in the context of Psalm 8, which are an allusion to the famous *imago Dei* passage in Genesis 1:26–28.

The verb *exalt* (in v. 17), when applied to humans, recalls the act of God making humans a little less than God or gods (ʾ*elohim*). The "visit" (in v. 18) of God is an allusion to the special treatment of humans as exalted beings remembered daily by God, the Creator. As I have indicated elsewhere,

> *the poet's use of the tradition that human beings were created in the image of God suggests that Job is portrayed as a legendary figure who began with the assumption that a high potential for human beings was a living option in the distant past. The reality of Job's experience, however, reveals that God by his alien intervention has frustrated the potential of his creatures.* (Habel 1985, 165)

For Job, the *imago Dei* tradition is a false dream. The God who "visits" Job belittles rather than exalts, humiliates rather than glorifies, induces trauma rather than potential.

The Torment of a Trauma Sufferer

Job continues to confront God with his pain, the intense fixation of the divine stare on an innocent mortal. He then throws his innocence back in God's face.

He even accuses God of setting Job up to be a target for divine marksmanship, a celestial archer watching to find a sinner at whom he can fire poisonous arrows.

At the end of the first stanza of this chapter, Job closes with a provocative taunt, a confronting satire. One day God will be frustrated. Despite being the great Seeing Eye and Watcher of Humans, he will one day be searching for Job to make him miserable, but Job will not exist anymore. The implication is that God will become the miserable hunter with no Job to hunt.

Job's taunts suggest that his trauma eases for a moment during his experience of divine attack by contemplating a better life in the land of the dead. For a moment he revels in the claim that his death might bring frustration for the divine Eye on high.

A trauma reading of Job chapter 7 has, I contend, a number of implications for those of us who wish to relate dimensions of this text to theology, psychology, and spirituality, especially in the context of counseling.

In 7:11 Job exclaims,

> *I rail in the torment of my spirit!*
> *I complain in the bitterness of my soul!*

Job's cry of anguish reaches deep into his psyche, or in biblical terms, his *ruach* (breath/spirit) and his *nephesh* (inner self). The psychological dimensions of that angst are apparent in his experience of horrendous nightmares and cruel dreams. His inner being is traumatized both day and night.

The satirical reference to the *imago Dei* tradition illustrates how certain traditional theologies are thought to play a positive role in both understanding and counseling people with trauma. To assert that humans in pain should remember they have been created in the image of God does not necessarily provide comfort. On the contrary, the sufferer may experience the opposite understanding of his/her status before God and have a disturbing image of God. Humans in agony may feel like slaves, not God-like creatures.

Job does not experience his identity as being *imago Dei* (in the image of God), but as *imago servi* (in the image of a slave). Many a trauma sufferer may identify with Job's experience.

The significance of a trauma analysis of this text, however, moves beyond the psychological and theological to the spiritual. Job is depicted here as suffering spiritual abuse at the hands, not only of his counselors but also of God. We can identify "God Trauma," as spiritual trauma about God as well as trauma caused by God.

Job here experiences his God as a Seeing Eye and a Watcher of Humans, not a compassionate companion with a Listening Ear. Job feels spiritually abused by the one who ought to render spiritual support. Job is a tragic victim of trauma that affects his psyche, his theology, and his spirit.

CHAPTER 6

Counsel of Bildad

Job 8

The inherited spiritual truths
of most religious traditions
may be appropriated,
not only to sustain faith
and inspire ritual,
but also to provide a resource
for pastoral care
and trauma counseling . . .
often
with harmful outcomes.

BILDAD IS THE second of Job's counselors and would-be therapists. Unlike Eliphaz who claims to have a special revelation of
the truth, Bildad claims that truth resides with the fathers. In
line with the Wisdom tradition reflected in the early chapters of
Proverbs, truth is handed down and accumulated as Wisdom from
one generation of mentors to the next and taught by mentors or
Wisdom "fathers" who address their students as "sons" (Prov 4:1,
5:1, 6:1).

And many of these truths are captured in the form of proverbs
or parables, like the parable of the two plants in this discourse of
Bildad.

Adherents of the Wisdom School of thought did not expect a
direct revelation from their God as the prophets did. They gained

their Wisdom primarily from two sources, the truths handed down from the fathers in the form of proverbs, insights, or parables and the truths revealed in the way that nature functions.

I explored this understanding of Wisdom in my *Earth Bible Commentary* on Job (Habel 2014) and in my study on *Discerning Wisdom in God's Creation* where I stated,

> *In the Wisdom school, a person interested in becoming wise was expected to observe nature and understand its 'ways' closely. Following this practise, the individual may not only learn lessons about life, but also about the phenomenon itself, its 'way' or inner wisdom.* (Habel 2015, 21)

As one of the wise, Bildad claims to know the "truth of the fathers" and outlines a parable about nature that illustrates the truth about life itself and the God that he believes Job should be able to recognize.

Bildad does not respond, in this discourse, to the specifics of Job's traumatic outbursts in Job 7. Instead, he focuses on a traditional belief that El is a God of justice and duly rewards or punishes, a truth of the fathers that Job is expected to remember.

In a later context, Bildad also delights in providing a colorful portrayal of the plight and place of the wicked in the world (ch. 18). Initially, he claims that Job views his friends as nothing more than stupid cattle and that he is a raving fool who mauls himself. His trauma is viewed by Bildad as self-inflicted.

In the lengthy portrayal of the plight of the wicked that follows (18:5–21), Bildad declares that the light of the wicked is soon extinguished, that the wicked are trapped by snares and traps and that death terrifies the wicked. Bildad even claims that the memory of the wicked perishes, that they have no surviving offspring and that they dwell in a place where El does not dwell.

In the eyes of Bildad, the wicked are destined to experience violent trauma at the hands of the King of Terrors, but their name on Earth will soon disappear, a truth Job should recognize. In the background to Bildad's portrayal of the plight of the wicked is the Covenant God of Israel who inevitably brings judgment to the wicked.

In what is probably his final speech (25:1–6, 26:5–14), Bildad ignores Job's trauma and elaborates on the awesome mysteries of the God El, before whom a mortal is but a miserable worm (25.6). This later portrayal of El does not seem to match the image of a compassionate deity suggested here in Job 8. In the end, Bildad's covenant theology is exposed.

In the immediate context, however, Bildad tries to function as one of the wise, presuming to act as a mentor/father advising Job to learn from the truth of the fathers.

If we realize that Job represents a suffering Wisdom community, probably in postexilic Israel, it seems that the narrator deliberately creates the figure of Bildad to play the role of a traditional Wisdom counselor. If the suffering community is indeed a Wisdom community, they ought to be willing to listen to the counsel of someone who claims to be a Wisdom elder. In the portrayal of the narrator, Bildad tries to persuade the Wisdom community that the Wisdom truths of the fathers convey the same message as that of the covenant tradition of reward and retribution, a message that Job is driven to expose as false.

Plead for Mercy!

Bildad begins by alleging that Job's outburst is a "big wind," a lot of hot air, because, from his alleged Wisdom tradition, Bildad can ask,

> *Does El pervert justice?*
> *Does Shaddai pervert the right?* (8:3)

The designation of God as El Shaddai, an ancient title found in the Abraham narrative (Gen 17:1), suggests that the narrator may portray Bildad using a portrait of God from the ancient fathers whom they believed knew the truth about God.

As an aside, Bildad suggests, in the light of Job's claim to be innocent, that perhaps Job's children must have sinned and caused God to "dispatch" them. As a result, Bildad argues,

> *But you, if you go early to El,*
> *and implore the mercy of Shaddai,*
> *if you are pure and upright,*
> *then he will rouse himself for you*
> *and restore your righteous abode.* (8:5–6)

It may also be relevant that El, the God worshipped by both Abraham and the Canaanites, was understood to be a compassionate deity, not a God bent on retributive justice, like the Covenant God Moses knew, or the devious deity of the prologue.

In one Canaanite text (the Ugaritic Keret text) El is repeatedly called "The Kindly One, El, The Merciful." El reveals his purpose for Keret in a dream and promises him progeny. The moral aspect of the character of the ancient God El is seen in his directive for Keret to do no violence to a particular town (Gray 119). El is the compassionate Creator God of the father Abraham and the ancient Canaanites.

Because of El's compassionate nature, Bildad assumes that Job only needs to plead for mercy and his God would restore Job and his household. For Bildad, however, his God El is an ancient version of the Covenant God of restorative justice with a dimension of mercy rather than retributive justice with relentless punishment. As I explained earlier,

*For traditional wise men like Bildad, justice implies a
process of divine management which preserves a consistent
pattern of reward and retribution. He therefore looks for
something in Job's past which might offer a logical ground
for retribution and selects Job's children as the most likely
target.* (Habel 1985, 174)

It may be relevant also to recall that in the Prologue, the
narrator maintains that Job would rise early on certain feast days
and sacrifice a burnt offering for each of his children in case they
had sinned and "cursed God in their hearts" (1:5). The implication
is that Bildad is suggesting a similar resolution of Job's trauma.

The Truth of the Fathers

Bildad claims his teaching is grounded in the Wisdom of the
fathers, the truth that he believes has endured for many generations. He therefore confronts Job with the counsel,

> *Ask now of an ancient generation,
> and study the truth of the fathers.* (8.8)

The special significance of this declaration is that the truth
about God, humanity, and life on Earth is not necessarily a
prophetic revelation, a code revealed to Moses, or an insight
derived from recent experience. Job's beginning may have been
viewed as "small" according to Bildad (8:7), but the truth of the
fathers extends back to ancient generations. Since the legend of Job
is located in the patriarchal past, "ancient generations" may well
be understood to extend back into the primordial.

In view of this ancient enduring reality, people like Job and his
friends of the present generation amount to nothing but a shadow.

Unlike the ancient tradition of the fathers that guides the hearts of all generations, the recent experience of men like Job has no serious truth value . . . at least according to Bildad.

The truths of the fathers are identified as "the words of their hearts," which is equivalent to the truths that have been tested over time in the mind of the wise, remembering that in the biblical tradition the heart was believed to be the mind, the source of critical thought.

The Parable of the Two Plants

In this parable, Bildad recounts the Wisdom of the fathers derived from nature and handed down over the generations. Human beings can be compared to two types of plants, those that have shallow roots and die quickly and those that have deep roots that wind around rocks and flourish among the dust even in the hot sun.

Those with shallow roots are those people who "forget El" and become "godless." They inevitably find they are trusting in a "spider's house" that will not stand but will fall when they lean on it (Job 8:13).

Those with deep roots are those who trust in El and will survive all hardships, knowing that "El does not spurn the blameless" (8:20). Pivotal for an appreciation of this plant is the claim:

> *Such is the joy of its way,*
> *that from the dust it shoots up elsewhere.* (8:19)

The term "joy" may be somewhat ironic, but the term *derek* (way) is a technical Wisdom term for the innate capacity that gives an entity its identity and integrity (Habel 2015, 16). According to Bildad those, like Adam, who emerged from the "dust" of the ground, and who have sustained the integrity of the "way" planted within them, will survive. Bildad, alas, does not recognize that Job is one such person, even though he closes his discourse with a word of comfort: the blameless will celebrate with shouts of joy.

The counsel of Bildad highlights how those governed by the tradition of the fathers readily assume that the so-called "fathers" have all the answers relating to suffering, survival, trauma, and God. The alleged truth of the Wisdom fathers is here made explicit: those who are blameless and trust in their God will survive and ultimately flourish, like a plant with deep roots. Those who trust in their own experience will wither and die. Here the "truth" of the fathers is viewed as consistent with the faith of the covenant faithful.

This portrayal, however, reveals a comprehension of reality that is typical of many ancient biblical traditions—namely, that the world is dualistic in nature. That dualism, in texts like Job, is not confined to the realms of heaven above and Earth below but includes realms of society where the humanity is divided into the righteous and the wicked, the wise and the foolish, the faithful and the evildoers. And specific characteristics and destinies are associated with each category. The friends reflect this dualism as a truth of the fathers. The Wisdom narrator, however, portrays Job as daring to challenge this tradition.

CHAPTER 7

Facing an Angry Adversary

Job 9–10

> *God trauma may persist*
> *beyond a devastating response*
> *to tragic events*
> *to the perception of God*
> *as an intervening adversary*
> *intensifying*
> *the stress of prior*
> *traumatic moments.*

AFTER THE PRIOR outbursts of Job, he takes a massive leap. Leaving the trauma of potential death and the misery of being a human on Earth, Job contemplates litigation only to experience an even more powerful trauma, an experience I would designate as "God trauma."

Job begins by recognizing the apparent futility of taking God to court. A human could not possibly win a case against a God "who would not answer one charge in a thousand" (9:3). In spite of the folly of litigation, Job nevertheless explores what litigation against his divine adversary might be like, a litigation experience that is extremely traumatic.

Job ignores the counsel of his friends who have sought to make him realize not only that he is a sinner by nature but also that he and/or his family must have sinned to have provoked such disasters from a righteous God.

The narrator, it seems, not only empathizes with the extreme anguish of his distraught Wisdom community but also experiences a deep sense that the God they have known has himself been untrue to the eternal covenant established with the people of Israel. If their God has indeed broken the covenant, the narrator has Job seeking to confront their God: the elusive, angry adversary they once knew as their compassionate Creator.

The narrator, however, is so radical in his representation of his people, he even envisages Job taking God to court for breaking his covenant relations with his faithful servant and ultimately with the Wisdom community. But the very contemplation of such a subversive action only arouses new levels of fear and frustration.

The significance of the covenant context for appreciating the communal trauma of Israelite communities, such as the one Job represents, is outlined in the research of Balentine,

> *Hebraic legal materials, principally the Decalogue and the Book of the Covenant, provide an important index of ancient Israel's history and values. This is especially instructive when Israel's laws are examined in relation to what was likely its most traumatic experience: the mass deportation of the population to Babylon in 586 BCE. The presenting question in what follows is this: Does the formative logic of the covenant, by which God promises reward and threatens punishment, effectively use law to legitimate divine violence?*
> (2008, 216)

The Trauma of Facing an Elusive Adversary

Job begins (9:1–13) by describing some of the wonders of nature that he interprets as the wounds of nature—creation suffering unknowingly—from outbursts of divine terror.

The God trauma that Job experiences is, first of all, facing not only the harsh capacity of his God to overwhelm nature with terrifying wonders but also the utter frustration of never actually confronting this elusive power in person.

The God whom Job contemplates facing as his adversary at court and confronting with the truth of Job's angst is, in Job's experience, not only elusive but always angry. In Job's understanding, God is not only omnipresent and hidden but also omni-angry and unapproachable. Job is now depicted as contemplating litigation against an unseen destroyer whose anger reaches back to the primordial when he destroyed forces of chaos like Rahab.

The Trauma of Facing a Cruel Opponent

Job, however, does not cease trying to contemplate taking his divine adversary to court (9:14–21). Even though he knows he is innocent, Job has no way of confronting God with the charges that Job maintains he has against God. He is frustrated beyond belief!

The trauma that Job knows as he contemplates litigation would only be intensified, claims Job, if he did meet God in court. In court, his God trauma would be devastating and cruel. The whirlwind of God would, he believes, prevent Job from catching his own wind/breath. An ironic twist is reflected here in the language Job employs because the cruel "whirlwind" Job anticipates here is precisely the "whirlwind" that Job experiences when God does appear (38:1). Does that subsequent appearance also cause an additional God trauma for Job or was is it a form of "shock therapy"?

Job's image of his God is one of relentless cruelty and domination, even in court where justice is supposed to prevail. The God of covenant justice has become the source of unwarranted injustices, a God whom the traumatized Wisdom community apparently finds intolerable.

Given the trauma of his past experience of God, Job can only imagine being damned by his God, in spite of his innocence. His God, claims Job, "mocks the despair of the innocent" (9:23). In other words, Job not only experiences God trauma, Job also believes that God is laughing at the profound trauma that Job has known. Job suffers the trauma of being powerless in the face of an all-powerful unsympathetic God.

Trauma of a Case without an Arbiter

Job begins the next stanza of chapter 9 (vv. 25–35) by contemplating a way of trying to overcome his trauma and start again. After all, he now views his life as but a fleeting moment on Earth. But when he tries to escape, his sufferings overwhelm him.

Job assumes that with his God hounding him day and night, God has already declared Job guilty. The frustration of Job's struggle to escape God's apparent declaration of guilt by violating his covenant bond only intensifies the trauma. Even if Job were to try and cleanse himself of sin by washing himself with snow or purifying himself with lye, God would still plunge him into a filthy pit that covers him with the appearance of guilt.

Another dimension of Job's trauma is that his adversary at law is an elusive, invisible character who is divine and inaccessible, not human and accessible, someone whom he can face in a normal human court.

Job imagines a court in which there is a fair trial. Job would then be able to face his adversary without being intimidated by the terror that his presence imposes on Job. The trauma Job faces, however, includes the reality that there is no arbiter who has the capacity to stand between God and Job to prevent the terrifying encounter that would threaten Job.

The trauma the Wisdom community experiences must be one of comparable frustration without an arbiter to justify their cries of unwarranted cruelty, even though the narrator functions as a mediator of their voice through the character of Job.

Job's Rehearsal of His Case

Despite the God traumas that Job has experienced and the absence of an arbiter who could enable a fair trial before a God whom Job views as vicious and unfair, Job contemplates going to court and confronting his God.

Job imagines he is in court facing his divine adversary. His opening declaration challenges God to prepare his case.

> *I will say to God, "Do not declare me guilty!*
> *Let me know your suit against me."* (10:2)

Job then challenges God to consider why he should oppress the innocent and "smile on the counsel of the wicked." He even engages in a little sarcasm wondering why God, who is not a human being with a short lifespan, should spend his celestial years searching for Job's sins even though, deep down, God knows Job is not guilty.

Job's Charges against His God

Job's declaration of his charges against God (10:8–17) includes the testimony that God created Job with the intention of destroying him, that all the love God has allegedly bestowed on Job has remained hidden, that God is obsessed with discovering Job's sins, that God saturates Job with misery in spite of his innocence, that God hunts Job as if he were a lion, and that God finds witnesses against Job to prove his guilt.

Job concludes his imagined case against God with another challenging question that reflects Job's earlier trauma of contemplating the option of being stillborn and the option of contemplating suicide.

Job pleads for a few days of sunshine (10:20–22) when he can "smile a little" before entering the land of shadow, the land of the dead. Job's God trauma concludes with the utter frustration of no hope of a trial, no arbiter, no end to the terror of God's presence, and no chance of any happiness before Job dies.

CHAPTER 8

Counsel of Zophar

Job 11

> *Traditional Wisdom*
> *may be cited as a basis*
> *for trauma counseling,*
> *assuming the therapist has*
> *an appropriate understanding*
> *of the Wisdom of God*
> *that is accessible*
> *for trauma therapy,*
> *but as Zophar presumes. . . .*

ZOPHAR IS THE third of Job's counselors, a rather brash and sarcastic friend. His predecessors Eliphaz and Bildad claimed to know the truth of the situation, Eliphaz by virtue of a special revelation and Bildad because he claimed to know the truth of the fathers, the teaching of past Wisdom generations.

Zophar, it seems, implies that he is initiated into the esoteric mysteries of Wisdom that are normally beyond human reach. He presumes to know the hidden mind of God about Job's sins (v. 6).

Zophar goes beyond the approach of Bildad, who claimed to know the truths of the Wisdom fathers. Zophar claims to know the inside story on Wisdom and therefore to be able to expose Job's claims as pure bluff and to provide the necessary counsel for Job to repent of his excessive guilt.

In his subsequent speeches, Zophar revels in describing the world of the wicked, their fall, their food, and their future (ch. 20; 27:13–23).

Zophar also outlines the fate of the wicked in very rugged language, asserting that the wicked perish forever like their dung. Zophar seems to enjoy portraying not only the fate of the wicked but also the way the wicked "relish" the taste of evil, even though they are eventually forced to vomit their food.

> *The evil tastes sweet in his mouth*
> *and he hides it under his tongue.*
> *He relishes it, does not let it go,*
> *and savours it under his palate.*
> *The food in his bowels is turned*
> *to asps' venom within him.*
> *The wealth he gorges he vomits;*
> *El forces it up from his stomach.* (20:12–15)

In spite of evil being like delicious food, the principle of retribution plays its role, and the wicked human is forced by El to vomit his meals. Zophar then elaborates further on the disgusting digestive experiences of the wicked. He is forced to disgorge his gain. Why?

> *Because he oppressed and abandoned the poor,*
> *seized houses he did not build.* (20:19)

The future of the wicked is determined by the principle of retribution, a principle in line with the covenant theology of the preexilic and postexilic community of Israel. There is no escape because,

> *When his belly is full*
> *God will send his fierce anger upon him,*
> *and rain it upon him as bread.* (20:23)

These disasters, according to Zophar, are God's portion for the wicked human. Cruel retribution is the inheritance ordained by God.

At first glance it might appear that Zophar is a member of the Wisdom community to which the narrator belongs. Zophar claims to know the mysteries of the Wisdom tradition that are crucial for Job's healing and ultimately for restoring the traumatized Wisdom community.

Upon closer investigation, it becomes apparent that Zophar claims to possess superior knowledge to that of Job, of the narrator, and of the local Wisdom community. Zophar is a representative of the traditional "right-wing" community of Israel that assumes to know the truth about the nature of God, including the inherent Wisdom of God.

The narrator represents an alternative empathetic perspective that refuses to automatically accept that image of a God in which the hidden Wisdom of God is consistent with the reward and retribution orientation of the Covenant God of Israel. Job is the voice for that "subversive" alternative perspective that the narrator is announcing to challenge the suffering community with which he identifies.

Zophar's "Wise" Rebuke

Zophar begins by confronting Job with a blunt rebuke. He accuses Job of boasting with an avalanche of words that may silence humans. Job may claim that his "teaching is pure" and that his innocence should be apparent. But, claims Zophar,

> *Oh, if only God would speak*
> *and talk to you himself.*
> *He would expand the secrets of wisdom,*
> *for there are two sides to understanding.*
> *Know that God exacts from you,*
> *less than your guilt demands.* (11:5–6)

Zophar contends that even though there may be two sides to understanding—the hidden and the evident—Zophar believes he knows the evident side: Job is guilty and deserves even more suffering or trauma than he has experienced to date. There is no need for the litigation Job has proposed. Job is obviously guilty!

The exploration of Wisdom at this point in the book of Job may seem surprising. I have explored the significance of Wisdom as a diverse cosmic reality in my volume on *Finding Wisdom in Nature* (Habel 2014). Zophar's concept of Wisdom is, however, limited and somewhat misleading. As I indicated,

> *According to Zophar, God's wisdom has secrets, a hidden dimension that humans cannot discern with natural intuition or uninitiated mind. . . . Zophar is not concerned about wisdom in the domains of the cosmos (as in Job 28), but how the distant mind of God is working in relation to Job's case. He applies his doctrine of the hidden wisdom of God in the mind of God to Job's situation and delivers a backhanded indictment (v. 6c).* (Habel 2014, 67–68)

Zophar's approach highlights human ignorance in the face of God's transcendent knowledge. Job's trauma, however, is not alleviated by Zophar's counsel—Job is viewed as an ignorant fool, like a "wild ass"!

Zophar's Inscrutable Deity

Zophar has an image of God as an inscrutable being whose hidden mystery/Wisdom is far beyond the reach of human intellect and research.

> *Can you find the mystery of Eloah?*
> *Can you find the limit of Shaddai?*
> *It is higher than heaven—what can you do?*
> *It is deeper than Sheol—what can you know?*
>   (11:7–8)

The verbal root of the noun for mystery (*cheqer*) refers to researching a matter and probing its depths (cf. 28:3) in accordance with the principles of the Wisdom School of thinking. "Limit" refers elsewhere to the depths an explorer may probe in mining the Earth (28:3) and to the outer limits of Earth where darkness and light meet (26:10). God alone has probed the depths of Wisdom (28:27).

Zophar claims that the profound Wisdom of God is beyond the capacity, even of the wise, to be discovered and known. Yet Zophar claims that his God identifies deceitful men and discerns evil, a truth Job should appreciate. Otherwise, Job is but a fool like the wild ass in a famous Wisdom proverb,

> *A hollow mortal will become wise,*
> *when a wild ass's colt is born human!* (11.12)

Job's trauma would not be alleviated when his friends declare him to be not only guilty but also dumb as a wild ass! Zophar sees no possibility that an addle-brained fool like Job could be transformed into a wise, intelligent human.

Zophar's Wisdom Counsel

Despite his portrait of God's Wisdom as inaccessible, Zophar offers his personal Wisdom as to how Job should respond to his situation. In the eyes of Zophar, Job's recovery from his trauma involves turning to God with penitent outstretched hands, cleansing his personal life of all existing iniquities, removing all lies and wrongs surviving in his household, and receiving the cleansing forgiveness of God.

If Job takes these steps as a penitent sinner, then his trauma will disappear, or in the words of Zophar, "You will forget your misery!" (11:16).

Zophar expands on what Job will experience when his trauma disappears. Zophar claims that Job will trust in his God because there is hope, will search and find rest, will not be terrified, and will be the center of attention for good.

Zophar's portrayal of the omnipresence of God as distant, invasive, elusive, and unknowable by ordinary mortals raises questions about the nature of this God of Wisdom being affirmed. In the development of the plot of the book of Job, we will be privileged to encounter an alternative Wisdom God introduced by the Wisdom narrator and experienced by Job.

CHAPTER 9

Facing God Creating Chaos

Job 12

God trauma may,
ironically,
also be experienced by individuals
who misread
the innate Wisdom of God in nature
and discern Wisdom
as a force that creates chaos.

IN THE PREVIOUS chapter, Zophar, an alleged disciple of the Wisdom tradition, articulates how he believes the distant mind of God is working in relation to Job's case and applies the doctrine of the hidden Wisdom of God in the mind of God to Job's situation. Zophar has an image of God as an inscrutable being whose inherent divine Wisdom is beyond the reach of human intellect. Zophar implies that if Job is to appreciate his situation, Job needs to recognize the mystery of God's Wisdom as a profound, invisible force in his crisis.

Job responds by rendering a satirical portrayal of inherent divine Wisdom that leads him to "grope in the darkness."

To appreciate this portrayal of God's Wisdom, we need to recognize that the narrator has depicted Job rendering a doxology, like those appearing in the Psalms and Proverbs, but with a brutal satirical twist. Especially relevant is the doxology of Psalm 104 that begins,

O YHWH, how manifold are thy works;
in Wisdom thou has made them all. (104:24–30)

As a satire on a doxology, Job's portrayal of inherent divine
Wisdom is tantamount to a disclosure of that dimension of a God
that his friends rendered inscrutable and, ultimately, not only
powerful but also positive.

While the "conservative" Wisdom God of Zophar suggested
representatives of the Israelites' postexilic community who were
ready to counsel the traumatized Wisdom community with a
superior understanding of the Wisdom of God that ought to
cause Job to repent, the response of Job probably represents
members of the traumatized Wisdom community who are still
struggling with their traditional understanding of the Wisdom
of their God.

In other words, the narrator preserves the pain and
complexity of the profound struggle for the suffering Wisdom
community to move from traditional fixed images of God as a
Covenant God, or even a popular inscrutable Wisdom God, to a
bold, radical new experience of God that is ultimately liberating
and healing.

Fools for Friends

Job begins and ends his portrayal of Wisdom by rebuking his
friends, claiming, in a sarcastic blast, that Wisdom will die with
them.

Job closes this speech (13:1–5) by declaring he plans to state
his case before Shaddai and pursue his suit with El (13:3). But as
for his friends, he contends, they fabricate lies and would be better
friends if they remained silent.

Wisdom in Nature

Upon first reading, it may appear that Job is aware of the positive force of innate Wisdom in nature that is described later in Job 28, a life force I have explored in detail elsewhere in my volume on *Discerning Wisdom in God's Creation* (2015), and again in *The Wisdom Trinity* (2021).

A close examination of Job 12:7–9 reveals that Job is appealing to the innate forces of nature to testify to their cruel treatment by the God of Wisdom, not to celebrate Wisdom's innate presence. In the mind of Job, nature also knows the trauma he has experienced at the hands of the God of Wisdom.

> *Ask the cattle and they will instruct you,*
> *the birds of the sky and they will tell you,*
> *or speak to the earth and it will instruct you,*
> *the fish of the sea and they will inform you.*
> *Who among all these does not know,*
> *that the hand of Eloah has done this?* (12:7–9)

In the experience of Job, the Wisdom of God's cruel ways is known to all the creatures and domains of nature. This dimension of Wisdom as a force of chaos is, in Job's eyes, also innate in creation. It does not come with age (12:12). Its cruel ways are known not only to Job, according to Job, but also to the land and the creatures of the land. What happens in nature does not alleviate Job's trauma.

In effect, the trauma experiences of Job, and ultimately of the Wisdom community Job represents, are so devastating and destructive that they eventually begin to undermine the basic Wisdom beliefs of their Wisdom School tradition. Job portrays a traumatized Wisdom community whose resilience is being depleted by deep doubt.

God's Wisdom
A Doxology Satire

Verses 13–25 assume the form of a doxology, supposedly prais-ing God for employing Wisdom to establish order in nature and society. The opposite, however, is the intent of Job's doxology. Chaos is what results when God's power combines with God's Wisdom to control the cosmos. This destructive power is evident in the destruction of established orders of nature and society, in the depletion of society's leaders of genuine efficiency and in the disorienting of nations and their leaders.

In the depth of his trauma, Job experiences the Wisdom of God as a destructive force that creates chaos and despair. The harsh forces at work in nature are made explicit:

> *When he holds back the waters, they dry up.*
> *When he lets them loose, they overthrow the earth.*
> (12:15)

This destructive Wisdom of God not only causes chaos in nature, it also creates upheaval among the leaders of society and causes nations to be led astray. The result is that God exposes the depths of darkness and disorients the human mind. Job knows the dark trauma of those in authority because God has led them to experience this form of chaos as well.

It is one thing to understand how the traumatized Wisdom community that Job represents challenges the idolized image of the Covenant God of Israel. It is even more challenging to appre-ciate that the narrator, a Wisdom mentor, experiences profound trauma in relation to the inherent Wisdom of God that he has long accepted. His sense of the unwarranted intervention of God in history even extends to unwarranted intervention in nature.

Job's traumatic experience relating to inherent divine Wisdom raises questions about the dimensions of Wisdom innate in creation, questions that God asks Job to explore in depth during his tour of the cosmos in chapters 38–39. These chapters are a deliberate reversal of Job's satirical doxology in chapter 12.

CHAPTER 10

Facing God in Court

Job 13

*Human resilience to trauma
may stimulate
the courage of the sufferer
to confront God
with the truth of the tragedy
only to face the trauma
of a Covenant God
who terrorizes
presumptuous
plaintiffs.*

AFTER FACING THE trauma of potential suicide, the cruelty of confronting an aggressive God, the ugly experience of being a broken human, the debilitating counsel of his friends, and the trauma of a God who seems to exercise violent Wisdom, Job is portrayed as having the remarkable resilience to reconsider taking God to court, a decision that will confront him with a new range of potential trauma experiences.

In my original commentary of Job (in 1985), I explored the legal dimensions of the book of Job in detail. In short,

Job is not content with indulging his anger, berating his friends in typical disputation style, protesting his innocence, bewailing his miserable mortal condition, or exposing the

wanton cruelty of his celestial foe. Nor will he tolerate the course of action demanded by his friends.

Instead, he explores a bold alternative for resolving the conflict between himself and God. He contemplates and plans litigation, a court hearing in which both parties can be heard without fear of intimidation or false witness. Job begins rather tentatively with his planned lawsuit but progressively takes his life in his hands and eventually (in 31:35–37) challenges his adversary at law to appear in court with an appropriate writ. (Habel 1985, 63)

It is within the process of Job contemplating, exploring, planning, and finally drafting his court case against God that new dimensions of his trauma, and that of the narrator's community, are exposed.

The narrator portrays Job exploring the bold option of taking God to court a number of times in subsequent discourses. His plan for litigation is especially forceful in chapter 23, where he again declares he is ready to make his complaint. His dilemma is the elusive nature of his adversary:

> *Oh, if only I knew how to find him,*
> *that I could enter his dwelling,*
> *I would press my suit to his face,*
> *and fill my mouth with arguments.* (23:3–4)

Job is faced with the dilemma of locating God but cannot find him whether he goes North, East, South, or West. Yet Job has a sense that his adversary knows Job's whereabouts. Regardless of his innocence, Job believes he would not get a fair trial. Accordingly, Job cries,

> *Therefore, I dread his face;*
> *when I consider, I fear him.* (23:15)

As indicated in relation to Job's discourse in chapters 9–10, the narrator is so radical in his representation of his traumatized people, he even envisages Job taking God to court for breaking his covenant relations with his faithful servant and ultimately with the traumatized Wisdom community the narrator represents. But the very contemplation of such a subversive action only arouses new levels of fear and frustration.

In this discourse, the narrator takes another bold step and essentially declares that Job, as the representative of the traumatized community, is ready to take God to court to defend his innocence, even if it means being terrorized by God or dying in the process. The narrator seeks to reflect the extreme pain and anguish of his Wisdom friends who are traumatized by the unwarranted acts of injustice they have experienced and relegated to the category of "bad figs" that have been cursed by the Covenant God.

Pretrial Declaration

a.   Interrogation of Friends

Job begins his plan to take God to court, by interrogating his friends as potential witnesses. He confronts his friends to determine their stand on his forthcoming lawsuit.

> *Will you testify deceitfully in El's defence?*
> *Will you testify for him with prevarication?*
> *Will you be partial toward him,*
> *and play advocate for El?* (13:7–8)

Job, however, not only imagines the potential way that his friends may testify and defend their God, Job also wonders how they will fare when this God, who has traumatized Job, will actually confront the friends. After all, their arguments are nothing but ashes!

> *Will his presence not terrify you,*
> *and his dread overwhelm you?*
> *Your old axioms are proverbs of ashes,*
> *your defences but defences of clay.* (13:11–12)

The friends depicted here may represent members of the Israelite community who have returned from exile and remain righteous adherents of the Covenant tradition; they would readily testify before their God and remain ardent defendants, an option the Wisdom community would find unfair and cruel.

b.   Public Declaration of Intent

Before presenting his case before God, Job announces his intention of arraigning God, regardless of the consequences. Job claims he can wait no longer.

> *Yes, though he slay me, I will not wait.*
> *I will now argue my case to his face.* (13:15)

c.   Arraignment of God

Job announces that he is now prepared to present his case and articulate his arguments before God. He claims to have prepared his suit and publicly declared his innocence.

In anticipation of an arraignment of this nature, Job expects the possibility that a case before Job's God would lead to even more trauma experiences. To ward off these experiences, Job makes a crucial request,

> *Only grant me, El, two things,*
> *so, I need not hide from your face.*
> *Keep your hand distant from me*
> *and let your terror not intimidate me.* (13:20–21)

If God does appear in court, Job has to find a way not to face the terror of God that has, to date, traumatized Job. Job boldly confesses his willingness to face more trauma if he can but face God in court. Job then summons God to prepare his case against Job.

> *You summon me and I will be respondent,*
> *or I will state my case and you refute me.*
> *How many are my iniquities and sins?*
> *Inform me of my transgression and sin!* (13:22–23)

With a taste of satire, Job, who claims total innocence, summons God to enumerate his sins publicly in court.

d. Complaint against the Adversary

In spite of the courage Job seems to have summoned in order to declare his intention to take God to court, he closes this speech with a note of despair. His pretrial trauma surfaces again. Job accuses God of hounding Job as if he were an enemy of God. He even claims that God has drawn up a dossier of false charges that have led to a life of servitude. God is the source of Job's trauma.

> *You have drawn up bitter indictments against me*
> *and made me inherit the iniquities of my youth.*

You put my feet in stocks,
place my paths under surveillance,
and brand the souls of my feet. (13:26–27)

Job is treated as guilty, a prisoner chained in cruel divine punishment, even though he is innocent. The trauma he knows in this situation is like a "garment being eaten by moths" (13:28).

CHAPTER 11

Living without Hope

Job 14

> *The God traumas*
> *of meaningless existence,*
> *or human oppression by God,*
> *may be intensified*
> *when the sufferer reaches the point*
> *when there appears to be*
> *no hope whatsoever*
> *for mortals*
> *on this planet.*

AFTER FACING THE trauma of trying to find a way of taking God to court to confront his divine adversary and prove his innocence (ch. 13), Job relives the trauma of being a human being that he expressed so painfully in chapter 7. In that earlier outburst of agony, Job is portrayed as experiencing being a human being as a form of servitude with God as the divine taskmaster.

Here, Job's hope of returning from Sheol to face God in court at a designated time anticipates his later hope of seeing a redeemer handle his case in court even after he is dead (19:23–27).

This discourse reflects another wild hope embedded among expressions of deep despair and a sense of hopelessness.

In this discourse, the narrator seems to reflect the depth of despair that his Wisdom community is apparently experiencing. The community has reached a point where they seem to have no hope of revival from their condition as rejected members of the wider postexilic Israelite family, the rejected "bad figs" of Judah.

Despite the devastating trauma of his community, the narrator reflects a wild hope embedded among expressions of deep despair and a sense of hopelessness. The narrator refuses to succumb to total despair; he dreams of a new day for his people, even if it is portrayed as a bizarre return from Sheol.

Pretrial Desperation

a. The Pain of Being Human

In view of his perceived pathetic nature as a transient human being, Job questions whether he has a chance of facing God in court.

> *Will you open your eyes to this one?*
> *Will you proceed with litigation against me?* (14:3)

According to the retribution tradition of the friends, humans who are considered impure have no chance before God and their life is limited. So, pleads Job, stop being the celestial Seeing Eye and give us a chance to enjoy life. Job pleads with God to open his eyes and see the real Job, not the object of divine cruelty.

Job again has a sense that being a human being means experiencing life as a "hireling," a slave of God oppressed by the divine taskmaster. In chapter 7 he describes himself as a human being, not in the image of God (*imago Dei*), but in the image of a slave (*imago servi*).

b. The Hope of a New Life

In this stanza, Job explores the nature of hope using a plant analogy. Earlier Bildad compared one plant that withered and died with the godless and another plant having deep roots with the righteous (8:12–20). For Job, the polarity lies between mortals that wither like flowers and actual trees that have the "hope" to send forth shoots of new life. Mortals, it seems, have no such hope.

> *Now a tree has hope!*
> *If felled it will renew itself*
> *and its suckers not fail . . .*
> *But mortals die and reman lifeless.*
> *Humans expire, and where are they?* (14:7, 10)

The reference to God drying up the waters of a river may reflect the tradition of God drying up the Nile (Isa 19:5–10). Such bodies of water are considered eternal sources of life-giving water. Humans, however, dry up and disappear.

c.   The Hope of Suspending Litigation

In the midst of his trauma and the frustration of achieving an immediate court appearance, Job contemplates the option of a delay in the litigation process during which time Job would be hidden in Sheol and survive God's anger. Then a new court appearance date could be set.

> *If only you would hide me in Sheol,*
> *conceal me until your anger is spent,*
> *set a time to remember me. . . .*
> *You would summon me, and I would answer.*
> *You would long for the work of your hands.*
> (14:13–15)

The ultimate question Job is posing is whether there is a possibility that a human being, like Job, could enjoy a temporary asylum in Sheol and wait until God's anger against him was spent.

Then he would rise from the land of the dead at a designated date
and be free to proceed with his lawsuit against God.

d. A Cry of Frustration

Job closes this speech with a cry of frustration claiming that God
"destroys the hope of mortals." This is the God who causes the
trauma of helpless mortals and leaves them without hope. In this
cry, the severe pain and anguish of Job's trauma is apparent. God
overpowers mortals, humiliates them, and leaves them forever in
pain with endless posttraumatic stress.

The deep trauma Job understands is both suffering in the body
and mourning in the soul, biblical language for deep depression.
At this point when Job experiences profound pretrial trauma, the
reader is left wondering how he might ever overcome this extreme
angst and eventually face God.

In this discourse, we again discern how people suffering the
trauma of deep depression, during which there seems to be no hope
for future help or healing, may have wild dreams of resolution that
defy the sufferer's experience of reality.

In this wild dream we encounter the hope of rising from the
dead to celebrate new life—not in the later sense of resurrection
but in the hope of experiencing a direct encounter with God that
will result in healing for the traumatized community. The frustration of seeking to fulfill such a dream only intensifies the stress
of the trauma, especially God trauma.

CHAPTER 12

Facing "Bloody Murder"

Job 16–17

> *Trauma experiences*
> *are often emotional,*
> *psychological, spiritual, or social.*
> *They may also become experiences*
> *that transform the body*
> *into a battered pile of misery,*
> *an excruciating combination*
> *of aches, pains, and agony,*
> *an experience of*
> *bodily trauma.*

DESPITE JOB'S EARLIER anguish about facing God in court, his friends continue to rave on about divine retribution and the fate of the wicked, assuming Job must ultimately be one of them, Job's trauma about appearing in court only intensifies.

He now reflects on the very nature of the God who has brought him nothing but despair, to say nothing of the disgusting mockery of his friends. Amid all this agony, Job has a moment of hope—a *post-mortem* advocate who hears Earth crying "bloody murder."

In previous discourses, Job portrays God as a cruel adversary who terrifies him with nightmares (7:13–14) or makes him a target (7:20) with his arrows (6:4). In this discourse, however, the divine enemy is tantamount to a murderer whose anger rages against Job until he is killed—the innocent victim of God's relentless fury. God is the guilty party in the mind of Job.

A significant feature of trauma analysis is to recognize the use of somatic expressions and metaphors, or somatization. Somatization involves the articulation of personal and social distress through the medium of the body.

> *Loss, injustice, failure, conflict—all are transformed into discourse about pain and disability that is a metaphor for discourse about the self and the social world. The body mediates the individual's perception, experience and interpretation of problems in social life.* (Kleinman 51)

In this discourse of Job, we recognize the use of numerous somatic metaphors and idioms to highlight the intense agony of the social situation of the isolated Wisdom community.

Significantly, the ultimate source of this bodily anguish is the God El. Earlier Job had complained about violent nightmares (7:13–14) and the experience of this God as an angry adversary (ch. 9). In this discourse, Job is portrayed as suffering a range of bodily injuries at the hand of God, injuries that are finally tantamount to murder.

It is significant that the Wisdom narrator does not confine his portrayal of the suffering Wisdom community to social, psychological, or spiritual factors, but is also ready to depict his people as the victims of excruciating bodily aches and pain.

Job's Complaint against His Friends

Job begins again by exclaiming that his friends' arguments are nothing but hot air, arguments he could match but now withholds because that would mean but temporary relief.

Job also seems to imply, ironically, that if he changed places with his friends, he could do a much better job of providing comfort. He could shake his head in sympathy and console. The sympathy of his troublesome comforters, however, is too superficial to handle Job's trauma.

Later in this discourse, Job again complains about friends who do not accept the truth of his claims of innocence. He declares that he must stand surety for himself since God has prevented the friends from gaining a genuine understanding of Job's situation. Job demands that God not "exalt" his friends because God has no right to recognize their position as valid.

Job again describes the trauma of life in an unsympathetic community of so-called friends using vivid terms that also relate to his physical condition. He is experiencing a bodily trauma that none of his friends recognize.

After reflecting further on how the so-called righteous people treat him, he closes by declaring his friends fools,

> But as for all of you, turn back! Come on now!
> I do not find a wise person among you. (17:10)

Job's Complaint against God as His Enemy

Job, once more, describes in uncompromising language the trauma God has caused him. God is experienced by Job in the turmoil of his trauma as a vicious enemy, a raging adversary who causes his whole being to become nothing but a shriveled rag that observers view as evidence of his guilt. Job experiences the fierce impact of the "Seeing Eye" above penetrating Job's whole self, including his battered body.

Job experiences these horrendous attacks from his divine enemy even though he claims, "there is no violence in my hands and my plea is pure" (16:17). There may be no violence in the hands of Job, but the bodily violence God has inflicted on Job is bloodcurdling, resulting in a deep physical and psychological trauma.

After such repeated experiences of vicious God trauma, it may seem virtually impossible for Job to find escape and healing of any kind. After such fierce attacks that challenge God's integrity, one might, like the friends, expect some kind of divine reproof or punishment. At this stage in Job's journey, however, he continues to recount his misery.

Job's misery affects all domains of his body, his gaunt appearance, his torn torso, his pierced kidneys and ultimately his spilled blood, a vivid somatic portrayal of the trauma experienced by a distraught community of the wise.

Job's Hope and Despair

In his previous cry of hope, Job dreamed of asylum in Sheol followed by a time appointed for post-mortem litigation and vindication (14:13–17). Now he envisages a new scenario: the blood that God has shed in his cruel acts of violence against Job will cry out for vindication, like the spilled blood of Abel (Gen 4:10).

> *O Earth, cover not my blood*
> *and let my cry have no place!* (16:18)

Job's hope is not that God would hear the cry of "bloody murder," but that there would be someone in heaven who would recognize the cry of innocent blood and act as Job's witness and arbiter in a celestial court.

> *Surely my witness is in heaven,*
> *he who can testify for me on high.*
> *Let him be my advocate, my friend before Eloah.*
> (16:19–20)

Job knows of no one on Earth who has any appreciation of his plight. In a moment of desperation, he dreams of someone in heaven who is watching, just as God and the Accuser were once watching, someone who can witness his innocence and testify on Job's behalf in a celestial court. This heavenly witness is not God as some interpreters say, but an advocate who can mediate between Job and God, the way an advocate would mediate between human beings.

His hope, however, is a momentary hallucination. Job knows his spirit is broken, his body is broken, and his life is almost spent. He expects the grave.

Job closes this discourse with a cry of abject despair, trauma without hope. All the days of his life that might turn night into day only eventuate in darkness. The outcome is that,

> *I must hope for Sheol as my home,*
> *spread my couch in darkness,*
> *call to the Pit, "You are my Father!"*
> *and say to the worm, "My Mother! My Sister!"*
> *Where then is my hope?*
> *My hope who can see it?*
> *Will it descend to Sheol?*
> *Shall we go down to the dust together?* (17:13–16)

For Job, at this point in his trauma journey, the Land of the Dead, the Pit, the world of Sheol, is his only hope. That realm will become his home, his family far from the Earth whom he dreamed would protest when they heard his blood crying to God above. Job's trauma, he expects, will accompany him to the realm of darkness below.

CHAPTER 13

Wild Hope of a Trauma Sufferer

Job 19

> *The innate resilience*
> *of people experiencing*
> *profound trauma,*
> *whether it be bodily,*
> *psychological, or spiritual,*
> *needs to be recognized*
> *before counseling efforts*
> *are made that may further*
> *the feeling of brokenness*
> *or despair.*

THE CELEBRATED LITERARY structure of this chapter has been recognized by numerous scholars. As I have indicated in my commentary (1985, 297), the literary design of this unit embraces more than the classic verses relating to the redeemer. This famous redeemer section (vv. 23–27) is clearly framed by two balancing pairs of verses (vv. 21–22 and vv. 28–29). Verses 22 and 29 relate to the friends assuming the same alien role as God the hunter when they "pursue/persecute" (*rdp*) Job. The redeemer that Job foresees stands in diametric opposition to role of the friends. They are accusers like God; the redeemer is the ultimate friend, defender, and advocate. The framework also makes it clear that God remains one of Job's pursuers.

Within the precise literary design of this discourse, we are confronted with the voice of Job faced with the trauma of being attacked by his friends and his God, a voice with which we are invited to empathize. Nevertheless, Job emerges with a moment of wild hope.

In his previous discourse, Job had the fleeting hope that the blood, which God had shed in his cruel acts of violence against Job, would cry out for vindication like the spilled blood of Abel (Gen 4:10).

> *O Earth, cover not my blood*
> *and let my cry have no place.* (16:18)

Job's hope was not that God would hear the cry of his blood but that there would be someone in heaven who would recognize the cry of innocent blood and act as Job's witness and arbiter in a celestial court.

> *Surely my witness is in heaven,*
> *he who can testify for me on high.* (16:19)

In this discourse (in ch. 19), Job again dreams of a day when someone will rise to his defense, even if Job has already died. Earlier in chapter 14, Job has the wild dream of waiting in Sheol and then returning to the land of the living to face his divine adversary in court.

The narrator of the traumatized Wisdom community has Job take another leap of faith to inspire hope among his people. He begins portraying, through the figure of Job, how his isolated community feels abandoned by the wider community of faith, its prophets, priests, and elders, a community that has no sympathy whatsoever for the broken Wisdom family.

The narrator also envisages his community reaching a point where they feel all but deceased and obliterated from the face of

Earth. Nevertheless, the narrator inspires his community to dream of a day when, against all local expectations, the deadly treatment they believe they have received at the hands of the Covenant God and his so-called faithful defendants will be publicly proclaimed in heaven.

The narrator even has Job believe that there is someone in heaven with the integrity to believe Job and prove his innocence. That such a "redeemer" exists in heaven is also a bold expectation. After all, neither the God of unwarranted disasters nor the Accuser who provoked God to permit these disasters would hardly be expected to intervene on Job's behalf.

Yet, beyond the Covenant God and the God of unwarranted disasters, the narrator has Job expecting an unidentified power to intervene that will enable Job to "see" a different God, face to face. The way in which that hope is finally fulfilled for the traumatized Wisdom community is a consummate leap of faith by the Wisdom-oriented narrator (42:5).

The God Trauma Continues

After railing against his friends for abusing him with their arguments (19:2–5), Job again screams about the violence that God has inflicted on Job. Even if Job makes this violence public, his hope of litigation remains futile (19:6–7).

Job claims that his God has blocked every pathway with darkness. Job has no place to go to find access to a court where he could face his adversary and present a case against him. Job's litigation trauma is one of absolute frustration.

In addition, Job believes that God has destroyed him in many other ways. Job feels that God has uprooted his hope as if he were nothing but a tree. God is not only an adversary, God is tantamount to a relentless enemy (19:11–12).

The Experience of Total Isolation

The desolation Job feels is not confined to the trauma he experiences at the hands of God and his celestial army. Job's family, friends, and relatives have all deserted him (19:14–18).

Job's isolation is made unbelievably miserable because everyone he has known, whether friends or relatives, young or old, have not only abandoned him but also abused and rejected him (19:19).

The trauma of Job is experienced as emotional anguish, social alienation, and spiritual brutality. Job's world is portrayed as nothing short of hell on Earth.

The Wild Hope of a Redeemer

Deep in the depths of Job's misery, a wild hope erupts.

The prelude to this classic wild dream is Job's challenge to his friends asking, very sarcastically, for some pity because of God's cruelty. He wonders why they should hound him the way God has been pursuing him with horrors. Then comes, in the context of his frustrated efforts to summon God to court, a declaration that has influenced readers of Job, especially preachers and theologians, for centuries.

The declaration of hope begins with a dream that his litigation case could be inscribed on a stela for future generations to know the grounds for his claim of innocence (19:23–24).

Suddenly, amid his trauma, his agony, his isolation, and his hope of litigation, he has a wild dream of a Redeemer rising to be his advocate!

> I, I know that my redeemer lives
> and afterward he will rise on the dust—
> After, that is, my skin is peeled off,
> but from my flesh I will behold Eloah! (19:25–26)

This is probably the most famous verse from the book of Job, a verse cited by my Lutheran lecturers as proof that Job believed in the Redeemer known as Jesus Christ who "lives" because he has risen from the dead. That belief is preserved in an old hymn, "I Know That My Redeemer Lives" by Samuel Medley, we once sang at Easter:

> *I know that my Redeemer lives!*
> *What comfort this sweet sentence gives!*
> *He lives, he lives who once was dead;*
> *He lives, my ever living Head.*

Ironically, the comfort anticipated by Job was not related to the resurrection of a Redeemer, but a wild hope that after Job was dead, someone would rise on his dust and ashes to "redeem" him, to stand before Eloah and testify to Job's innocence.

I have earlier provided a detailed analysis of this passage and the diverse interpretations of recognized scholars (1985, 302–308). In brief, this text articulates the bizarre dream of Job that, even after he is dead, with no skin on his body, he would see Eloah.

The redeemer (*go'el*) is a significant figure in ancient Israelite and biblical tradition. The *go'el* refers to the next of kin who intervened to maintain the rights or preserve the continuity of the family. The responsibility of the *go'el* could involve avenging the blood of a murdered member of the family (Num 35:16–28; II Sam 14, 7, 11), redeeming someone from bondage (Lev 25:48–49), regaining family property to keep it within the family inheritance (Lev 25:25–28; Jer 32.6–11) and marrying a widow to provide an heir for her deceased husband (Ruth 4:3-6; cf. Deut 25:5–6).

Why does the narrator portray Job anticipating a *go'el*? Possibly because the term was associated with the role of a blood avenger and because earlier Job appealed to Earth not to cover his blood, as the violence he had experienced at the hands of God was viewed as tantamount to murder (16:18).

The *go'el*, however, also has legal connotations; Job not only considers God his adversary at law but also has not been able to summon God to appear in court. God is his accuser, his adversary, his enemy, his spy, and his destroyer. Against this opponent, Job needs a *go'el*, one who will take up his case and bring it before the court of heaven for public resolution.

In spite of his guilty appearance, the formidable nature of his adversary, and the absence of legal precedent, Job is convinced that a *go'el* will "rise up" in court, maintain his right to be heard, and represent him as a kinsman.

While some scholars have identified the *go'el* with God himself (Habel 1985, 306), the legal context clearly identifies God as the adversary, not the advocate. It seems logical that the *go'el* is a celestial figure like the celestial "witness" (16:19) or the "arbiter" (9:33) of previous wild hope speeches. The function of the third party is to guarantee that Job's case is given a hearing and to defend Job's innocence before a celestial court.

In the background lies the celestial Accuser who provokes God into permitting the deadly disasters that Job experiences (1:6–7).

There is some debate about whether the redeemer appears before or after Job is dead. The reference to his "skin peeled off" suggests that when Job has died, the redeemer will be alive to present Job's case. His wild dream is that even after his death, he will somehow behold his God, Eloah, and have his case heard (19:27).

Even though a *go'el* arranges a post-mortem trial and vouches for Job's innocence, Job would still like to confront his divine adversary in person and "see" him face to face, in spite of the terror Job has experienced (13:20–21).

He would then gain personal satisfaction from his ultimate vindication. Of course, Job does claim to "see" a God after the whirlwind experience, but the mode and context of that seeing is radically different (42:5).

Job closes this amazing outburst of wild hope by referring again to the way his friends have been pursuing/persecuting him (19:28–29). Job declares that he already knows a *go'el* will support his suit. When the dust settles, the friends will also know there is a time of judgment when all accounts will be settled.

CHAPTER 14

Living with Social Psychosis
Job 21

The psyche may be traumatized
not only by devastating losses
and brutal mistreatment,
but also by the agony of living
in an abusive society
where rich and
powerful wrongdoers
celebrate life to the full.

IN THE PREVIOUS chapters, the friends frequently outline the lives and fate of the wicked, often appearing to relish their destiny and doom.

Zophar, for example, follows the lead of Bildad (8:8) and Eliphaz (15:18–19) in appealing to the ancestors as the source of his teaching. He even claims his teachings are as old as Adam. The truth of the fathers is that the joy of the wicked is brief.

> *Surely you know this, that from of old,*
> *since humans were placed on the Earth,*
> *the joy of the wicked has been brief,*
> *the happiness of the godless one, but for a moment.*
> (20:4–5)

Zophar then describes the downfall of the wicked who perish "forever like their dung" and disappear like a vision in the night, bereft of all their wealth and power (20:6–11).

Zophar seems to salivate when he describes the way in which the wicked consume what is evil, relishing the taste and savoring the flavor in their mouths.

> *The evil tastes sweet in his mouth*
> *and he hides it under his tongue.*
> *He relishes it, does not let it go,*
> *and savours it under his palate.* (20:12–13)

Zophar moves beyond his colorful portrayal of the wicked who like to feast on evils and injustices and describes in rich poetic language the disasters awaiting the wicked once their "belly is full," disasters that penetrate a body filled with evils. The arrows of divine anger will pierce not only the stomach but also the back and the gallbladder (20:23–25).

Against Zophar's colorful portrait of the life and fate of the wicked, Job responds with a radically different picture. He sees the world of the wicked as free from fear of punishment, replete with a life of celebration and the anticipation of dying amid joy and companions. His experience may well be described as a trauma of social psychosis.

In this discourse, the struggle of the traumatized Wisdom community with the traditional covenant teaching of reward and retribution is apparent. The trauma portrayal of Job is designed to undermine the concept of retributive justice as pivotal for divine human relations and to explore a new paradigm for understanding the role of divine justice in the world of a community suffering trauma.

While the Wisdom community may not deserve to suffer at the hands of the Covenant God, the surrounding communities are filled with the wicked who go free of divine punishment regardless of their evil deeds. In the eyes of the narrator, the

Covenant God of reward and retribution deserves to be exposed as a false god.

The Happiness of the Wicked

Job responds to Zophar by telling him to "clap his hands over his mouth" and listen to Job's portrait of reality about the wicked. Job's version of the life of the wicked is the exact opposite of what Zophar described. According to Job, the wicked are happy, enjoy a long life, and live at peace.

The wicked, in the eyes of Job, are not only prosperous and prolific, they are also able to celebrate life with their children, as they sing, dance, and play music.

> *They sing to the timbrel and harp*
> *and rejoice to the sound of the flute.*
> *They spend their days in happiness*
> *and descend to Sheol in peace.* (21:12–13)

Even more significantly, Job claims that the wicked have the capacity to defy God and enjoy life without help from heaven. The wicked do not experience the misery and terror that Job has experienced. The wicked, in the mind of Job, are trauma free.

> *They say to El, "Leave us alone!"*
> *We do not delight in your ways.*
> *What is Shaddai that we should serve him?*
> *What do we gain by praying to him?* (21:14–15)

No Calamity for the Wicked

According to Job, the wicked rarely experience calamity. Job hears his friends suggesting that Eloah may have hidden his punishment from the sons of the wicked. But, says Job, if this God is true to his ways, he should exercise his retributive justice and force the wicked to drink "the wrath of Shaddai."

Job claims to know the thoughts of his friends who plot against him and refuses to recognize the evidence of those who travel the landscape.

The wicked enjoy a rich life without any retribution from God for all the wrongs committed. They have many who follow them and "spend days of happiness" before they die (Job 21:13). So, concludes Job, in a moment of utter disgust,

> *Why offer me empty comfort?*
> *Your answers are sheer perfidy!* (21:34)

It would seem that one suffering from cruel trauma can recognize what Job calls "empty comfort." The pain, it would seem, is not so much due to the sickening impact of the colorful portrayal of the worlds of the wicked but rather the harsh reality that retributive justice is understood to be at the center of God's relationship with humans. According to Zophar, the wicked will know an inheritance of disaster that is ordained for them. In the eyes of Job, the wicked seem to escape retribution and are blessed by their God.

Just as significant is that Job's experience of the lives of the wicked is tantamount to social psychosis. Job is not just describing the prosperous lives of the wicked, he is also facing the inner anguish and bitterness that he experiences as he describes the wicked celebrating life with song and splendor while he undergoes the agony of terrifying isolation and divine harassment. The wicked say to El, "leave us alone, so we can do our own wicked thing," while Job pleads with El to leave him alone and no longer intensify his inner pains.

CHAPTER 15

Unanswered Prayers

Job 23

> *God trauma*
> *may result in a deep depression*
> *that is experienced as total isolation*
> *in an overwhelming gloom,*
> *if God is experienced as*
> *an elusive*
> *inaccessible alien*
> *who never answers prayers.*

IN THE PRECEDING discourse, Eliphaz counseled Job to make a covenant with El and to receive instruction from his God so that he may know the way back to God. If Job does return to El, then Job will be rehabilitated. That was the covenant-oriented counsel of Eliphaz.

The irony of the wording of Eliphaz lies in his promise that if Job "sets his gold in the dust" (22:24), then El Shaddai will become his gold. In response, Job declares that if God actually tried him, Job would emerge "as pure gold" (23:10)

Essentially Job's response is that Eliphaz's counsel is ludicrous and as unhelpful as Eliphaz's previous attempts to counsel Job.

The narrator is aware of the efforts of his traumatized Wisdom community to obtain a response to its persistent prayers. In this discourse of Job, however, he is willing to expose the Covenant God of Israel as a futile source of support for his traumatized companions.

The narrator is bold enough to persist with undermining the Covenant God of Israel and prepare his community for a radical return to the roots of their Wisdom tradition. He is signaling a time for his people to search for meaning and presence from an alternative mode of communication. Traditional prayers addressed to an elusive traditional covenant deity in Israel remain futile.

Job's Quest to Find God

Job's opening cry is more than a cultic cry of lament (e.g., Ps 55:17). His complaint is a "defiant" (*meri*) call which in its present form is probably a pun on the adjective "bitter" (*mar*). The defiant dimension of his complaint results from the "heavy hand" of his adversary. Job wants God to meet him to press his suit against God. But God remains in hiding, ignoring Job's numerous challenges and accusations.

Job describes (in verses 4–7) what he believes would happen if he located God's heavenly court and presented his case before God. Job even claims he knows the wording of God's defense.

The Force of Job's Innocence

Why does Job claim that God's verdict ought to be in Job's favor and that God would not ever dare to ignore him or to use unwarranted force against Job?

Because Job is unequivocally upright, totally innocent, and free of blame. A God with any integrity could not possibly convict or punish him, yet such a God seems impossible to locate.

The Elusive Nature of God

Job's description of the elusive character of his God is a classic portrayal of human frustration in the face of unanswered cries to be heard by God. The issue for Job is to locate his God so that he can present his case, but God conceals his presence completely whether Job searches North, South, East, or West, traditional homes of the gods of the ancient Near East.

In one Israelite tradition, YHWH is located in "the far North" (Ps 48:3) and in another in Mount Zion. But for Job, God cannot be "discerned" in any of the extremities of Earth. In the Wisdom School, "discern" may involve seeing via observation, just as God "discerns" the presence of Wisdom by "looking" to the ends of the Earth and "seeing" everything under heaven (28:23–24). This makes it clear that Job wants to "see" God face to face, to confront God with his case rather than simply persist with frustrating prayers.

Ironically, Job does claim to "see" a God in his closing statement (42:5). In the midst of his present God misery, however, even locating God is but another God trauma.

Job's Calls for His Faithfulness to Be Tested

Job declares unequivocally, that if God dared to test Job in the way that metal was tested/tried in fire, God would find gold. Job is so convinced of his absolute integrity that he is willing to be tested in the all-consuming fire of God's holiness.

Job's daring challenge is grounded in his relentless claim that he is innocent and has followed the "way" of God unswervingly. The "way" (*derek*) not only is associated with the quest motif (28:7) but also refers to the innate character or nature of an entity. Job claims that God has hidden Job's "way" and made life meaningless (3:23).

In sheer contrast, Job claims to have kept to God's "way" without swerving. Job claims to know God's way even though ironically, God himself remains hidden and has hidden Job's way.

Job's Ominous Gloom

Despite Job's bold claims and persistent cries, God leaves Job totally frustrated because God, it seems, has the devious capacity to do what he chooses, decree what he likes, and abandon whomsoever he chooses.

The outcome of Job's unanswered pleas, screams, challenges, and hopes is sheer dread, terror, and darkness. The portrayal of this God trauma is one of ominous gloom without an answer from an elusive, terrifying deity.

CHAPTER 16

Oath before a Heartless God

Job 27

*The resilience
of the trauma sufferer
may even extend to
a bold declaration and exposure
of the persistent source
of the suffering
as an unforgivable enemy.*

AFTER 24 CHAPTERS of dramatic and vehement interchange—both between Job and his friends, as well as between Job and the God whom Job believes has been hounding him with horrors—Job makes a final declaration of innocence, a bold oath of integrity.

This oath is the culmination of the first half of the book of Job, a lengthy half in which God trauma is dominant and in which all the dimensions of life, relationships, hope, and faith are ultimately viewed from a negative traumatic perspective. Job sees no hope of healing in the counsel of his friends, in the presence of an all-powerful supposedly wise God or an arbiter who could prove Job's innocence in court.

Despite every effort to break his spirit and make him confess, Job concludes with a relentless claim of innocence, righteousness, and integrity.

The preface to Job's bold oath before God in chapter 27 is to be found in the discourse of chapter 23 where Job is totally

frustrated by the fact that he cannot actually locate God so that
he can confront him. As he cries,

> *Behold, if I go East—he is not there!*
> *West—I do not discern him.*
> *North—in his concealment I cannot behold him.*
> *South—he is hidden and I cannot see him!*
> (23:8–9)

Job dreads facing this elusive God dwelling in a world of
ominous gloom. In this discourse in chapter 27, however, Job
formulates his oath of integrity regardless of the consequences.

In the speech of chapter 27, which follows, I have included Job
26:1–4, a fragment of an earlier speech that seems to have been
misplaced, as I argue in my commentary (1985). Job's oath of integrity is framed by a sarcastic comment about his friends (26:1–4)
and an ironic declaration about his divine adversary, whom he here
designates as his enemy. Job's relationship with his God seems to
have reached the depths of darkness and desperation. Job is faced
with a heartless God. The later half of Job 27 (vv. 13–23) seems
to be a displaced speech of Zophar in which he again delineates
the fate of the wicked.

The narrator makes it clear, via the allegations of Job, that
the wider Israelite community, represented by the friends, have
provided no genuine support for the traumatized Wisdom
commentary to which the narrator belongs. All the arguments of
the covenant theology of Israel have proved weak and useless. More
specifically, they have offered counsel that has incorporated no
genuine Wisdom. This allegation exposes the traditional accumulated Wisdom of the elders proffered by Bildad and the inherent
divine Wisdom endorsed by Zophar and declares them an insult
for the traumatized Wisdom community whom Job represents.

Friends without Wisdom

In his closing comments of part I of the book, Job accuses his unsympathetic friends of trying to offer counsel "without having Wisdom." This accusation anticipates the lead question in the narrator's bold introduction to part II (ch. 28), namely, "Where can Wisdom be found?"

With a taste of bitter sarcasm, Job laughs at the pathetic attempts of his friends to support him when they are tantamount to powerless fools. They attempt to counsel Job in the midst of his trauma but fail miserably because they have no Wisdom.

The arguments of the friends are but hot air that assists no one!

The God of Job's Oath

In line with the tradition of Abraham, Job swears his oath by El, also known as El Shaddai. Job identifies this God as the cruel source of the terrors that embittered his soul and as the deity who, in spite of Job's unjustified traumatic experience, has prevented him from proceeding with litigation to prove his innocence.

The God of Job's oath is not the YHWH of the Mosaic tradition but bears the name of the ancient Creator Spirit, the Canaanite God of Melchizedek, who blessed Abraham and by whom Abraham swore. Whether the narrator is making this connection is not clear, but the oath of Job is in line with the history of oaths in the ancient world of the wise (Habel 2018, ch. 3).

"As El lives" is a standard formula introducing an oath (I Sam 14:39, 45; II Sam 2:27). Traditionally, the deity named in the oath formula is called on to curse the speaker if the oath is not true. Job's oath is the last resort of a desperate victim. The irony of this passage is that Job swears his oath before an imaginary court by the name of the very God who has denied him litigation.

Presumably this oath is designed to provoke the God who is supposed to be the guarantor of justice. By swearing by the life of El, Job takes the most powerful means at his disposal to force God to act. The onus is now on God to respond. Job's oath and God's silence, it seems, even provoke Elihu to be an arbiter and act on God's behalf (34.5–9).

Job's Oath to Tell the Truth

In the parenthesis (27:3) between the oath formula and the content of the oath, Job declares that he will stand by his oath as long as he lives. Ironically, the breath that enables him to live is identified as "the Spirit of God," the very God who caused his bitterness of spirit. Though bitter in soul (v. 2b), Job takes his oath of integrity as one being of "sound mind."

The substance of Job's oath is that he will tell the whole truth and nothing but the truth.

The idiom "far be it from me" is a serious formula that carries with it a self-deprecation. It is tantamount to sacrilege not to speak the truth of the declaration involved. Basically, Job is saying under oath, "May I be damned if I declare you to be in the right." Job is not willing to concede that ultimately God may be in the right. Nor is Job willing to forgive God. It is probably this act of declaring God guilty so that Job might prove his own innocence, that provokes God to challenge Job a second time from the whirlwind (40:8).

The noun "integrity" (*tumma*) sums up Job's claim of innocence and righteousness in his relationship with God. In the prologue, Job is declared a blameless man with integrity (2:3, 9). Now his gaunt appearance seems to testify against him. Nevertheless, Job claims his conscience is clear and his motives pure.

Job's Enemy

In his closing declaration, Job takes another risk and speaks about his "enemy." Job, it seems, is talking about God, the one who has attacked Job and mutilated his soul. God is the "foe" (*tsar*) who has attacked Job viciously (16:9; 19:10–12; 13:24). By wishing that his adversary at law would suffer the same fate as "the wicked," Job heightens the polarity between himself as the innocent party and God as the guilty one.

God had treated Job "as if" he were one of the wicked by afflicting him with endless trauma. Now Job is wishing the same suffering on his adversary. Job is envisioning his God suffering trauma with no deity ready to heed his cries for help.

A Closing Cry

Job adds to his earlier oath of integrity a closing declaration that he has indeed told the truth about his enemy, his God, El Shaddai, the truth about all the suffering Job has experienced unjustly as a man of integrity.

He even declares that his friends have "seen" everything that has happened and should not speak "nonsense/vanity" (*hebel*). In the context of the Wisdom School jargon, the one who "sees/ observes" a reality or a situation is one who sees the truth, speaks the Wisdom that has been discerned. Job's friends, however, speak nothing but "nothing" (*hebel*) (Eccl 1:2).

It is significant that the closure of Job's extended cries of agony and pain reveals that the trauma sufferer does not necessarily surrender into an alcove of despair. Instead, the integrity of the person in pain may be expressed not only by a desperate uncompromising declaration of injustice but also by a willingness to confront the source of his/her angst with a dangerous naming of the adversity as an "enemy" that deserves damnation, even if that enemy is experienced as God himself.

Job may have begun his outcries with "Damn the day I was born." He closes with a bold outcry, "Damn the deity who caused my trauma."

Wisdom therapy, it seems, allows the trauma sufferers to vent their feelings of injustice, agony, and intimidation in the most forceful manner before confronting the surprising alternative of Wisdom as a way of healing. This outcry may well be recognized as the beginning of the process of healing.

II

Wisdom Therapy
Job 28–42

STAGES ON THE journey of Wisdom therapy embedded in the book of Job may be discerned in both parts of the book of Job. While part II of the book commences with the Wisdom Manifesto (ch. 28) and leads to the intervention of the Wisdom Therapist (ch. 38), part I (ch. 1–27) records what may be designated as preparatory stages. These include the following:

Preparatory Stages

Stage 1
Ask the Eternal Why

After emerging from his traumatic experience of horrifying loss and family tragedy in which Job expressed a pious form of trauma denial, Job enters the first stage of his trauma journey as such and begins with what is often designated "the eternal why." Job asks why he was born and forced to live in misery.

Above all, he asks why a hedge has been planted around him so that he sees no "way"—no meaning, purpose, or direction in life.

Job knows the God trauma of meaningless existence, but he dares to ask the eternal why. The trauma community that Job represents is moved by the Wisdom narrator to ask the same question.

To ask "the eternal why" activates the spirit of the trauma sufferer to take even bolder steps— in contemporary terms activates the stress hormones in the mind, or in Wisdom School terms awakens the incarnate Wisdom in the heart.

Stage 2
Scream Bloody Murder

Contrary to many traditional therapy approaches, Job moves beyond questions of why or calls for compassion to screams and violent outbursts of anger. In Job 16, Job declares that his screaming is also a result of his potential "bloody murder" (16:18). Job's screaming implies that those who suffer trauma have not only a right to question their loss but also a right to scream. Job screams in numerous ways in numerous chapters, screams directed at the wrongs in his life, the counsel of his friends, the bitterness of his spirit, and the cruelty of his God.

Job knows the God trauma of facing "bloody murder," and he dares to scream at God. Through the voice of Job, the narrator frees his traumatized community to scream "bloody murder" in the face of the Covenant God whose harsh ways the community has been expected to endorse.

To scream in the face of God may also be therapeutic when the distraught trauma sufferer or community can discern no way to overcome the overwhelming stress of a meaningless existence and a God who imposes or allows unwarranted disasters.

Stage 3
Test Your Old Beliefs

In the midst of the screaming about what has happened and how it creates havoc in the soul, the innocent sufferer, like Job, may legitimately have doubts about the God whom he or she has come to know according to a specific tradition.

Job challenges the very idea that God is a constant compassionate and caring companion. In particular, he challenges the reality of a righteous God who is renowned for his fair administration of reward and retribution. He even accuses his God of being a Seeing Eye who relishes the sight of Job's trauma.

Job knows the God trauma of God as a virtual enemy, but he dares to challenge God's integrity. The narrator, through the agency of Job, supports the struggle of his traumatized community to come to terms with a Covenant God committed to living with a doctrine of reward and retribution.

To doubt traditional ways of understanding God can also be viewed as therapeutic, especially if one belongs to the Wisdom School that is known for testing the truth in the domains of reality.

Stage 4
Take a Leap of Faith

When the God of traditional values seems to be nothing short of an adversary or even an enemy, the trauma sufferer may contemplate suicide. Alternatively, he or she may dare to take a bold leap of faith and confront that God with a barrage of accusations or an attempt to take that God to court to reveal that God's guilt. Job contemplates that leap of faith and faces endless frustration until the healing process begins and he formulates in writing his declaration of innocence.

Job knows the God trauma of facing an elusive adversary, but he dares to take an oath to confront his God in court. The decision of Job to record his experiences in writing is a precedent that the Wisdom narrator introduces to a traumatized community reluctant to make their faltering faith public.

The stage of challenging prior traditional understandings of God prepares the way for the introduction of existential Wisdom and Wisdom therapy to guide Job and the traumatized Wisdom community on a journey toward healing.

Interactive Stages

Stage 1
Go Back to Wisdom School

After the preparatory stages of part I, the narrator takes Job and the Wisdom community he represents back to face the Way of Wisdom. That mystery is encompassed in an ancient poem that may well be designated a Wisdom Manifesto (ch. 28). In that declaration, we are confronted not only with the science of how to find existential Wisdom but also with a God whom the wise recognize as the original Wisdom Scientist. This God is a far cry from the perception of the Covenant God found in part I of this volume.

The healing journey begins when the trauma sufferer goes back to Wisdom School, meets the original Wisdom Scientist, and discovers the way to find Wisdom in a world of searching and suffering.

Stage 2
Tell Your Trauma Story

After screaming bloody murder in the face of God and yelling at his unfriendly friends, Job takes the bold positive step of drafting his life story as a respected and compassionate leader (ch. 29), enumerating a range of complaints against those in the community who have unfairly abused him, denying him any justice (ch. 30), and drafts a formal litigation with a series of oaths relating to his life as a righteous citizen who deserves justice (ch. 31).

An honest narration articulating the "before, during, and after" of the sufferer's trauma experience is also an important step on the journey of healing, a step that assists the resilient sufferer to look into the future even if that remains uncertain. By making their trauma experiences public, the traumatized Wisdom community, whom the narrator is challenging, has opened the way to discern a solution to understanding the nature of their plight and their God.

Stage 3
Recognize the Option of a Would-Be Arbiter

Unlike the preceding friends, Elihu formally assumes the role of an arbiter, a figure whom Job had envisioned for his court case with God. Elihu, the would-be arbiter, however, attempts to defend the traditional Covenant God rather than Job, assuming that God is the accused rather than the adversary in the court case Job imagines.

An arbiter, rather than a wise counselor, may clear the way for the final stage by eliminating a range of "healing options" that may still be considered reasonable by one who claims to know diverse modes of therapy.

Stage 4
Explore the Locus of Wisdom with the Wisdom Therapist

In this stage of the Wisdom therapy process, God, the Wisdom Scientist, becomes God, the invisible Wisdom Therapist, who takes Job with him deep into vast domains of the cosmos, free domains of the wild and imaginative domains of the primordial. God, the Wisdom Therapist, poses insightful questions that challenge Job to leave the dust and ashes of his trauma location and explore locations where the healing presence of innate Wisdom may be discerned in the complex design of the cosmos.

The Wisdom therapy of the book of Job involves experiencing provocative questions that challenge previous understandings of God and reality, questions that guide the trauma sufferer into amazing new levels of consciousness that overwhelm the cruel world of trauma.

The narrator has opened the doubting minds and the traumatized spirits of his Wisdom community to an amazing cosmos where mystery and meaning are embedded in the "ways" of Wisdom that function as healing pulses for all who are conscious of their spiritual presence in the cosmos.

Stage 5
Celebrate Healing

After acknowledging that his discernment about the amazing design of the cosmos was limited and that the cosmos was embedded with innate Wisdom forces, Job is ready to withdraw his court case against God, leave his trauma location identified with dust and ashes, and explore.

His supreme moment of healing is reflected in his famous statement: "I have heard of you with my ears, but now my eyes see you" (42:5). Job has gained a deep Wisdom consciousness about the presence of Wisdom active in the world that surrounds him. Job has discerned God as the Presence of Cosmic Wisdom.

He then proceeds to celebrate his healing with forgiven friends and family.

Wisdom therapy has the potential for the trauma sufferer to "see you," to discern innate Wisdom permeating and sustaining the domains of the cosmos.

The Wisdom therapy Job experiences also has the potential for the traumatized community whom Job represents to dismiss their Covenant God and be free to experience the Wisdom that the Wisdom God identifies operating in every component of the cosmos that surrounds them, a freedom that is worth celebrating.

CHAPTER 17

Wisdom Manifesto

Job 28

> *The ultimate questions*
> *in the Wisdom School*
> *are*
> *"Where can Wisdom be found?*
> *and who can find it?"*
> *The ultimate answers preserved*
> *in the Wisdom Manifesto*
> *are,*
> *"Wisdom is innate in the cosmos*
> *and God, the Wisdom Scientist*
> *has found it?"*

MANY SCHOLARS VIEW Job 28 as a surprising intrusion in the sequence of discourses exposing Job's trauma and the efforts of his friends to counsel and correct him. They argue that this poem is a secondary intrusion that interrupts the progression of speeches through the book.

Newsom argues that Job 28 is a distinctive genre that she designates a "speculative Wisdom poem," with features typical of the larger world of Wisdom literature. Her analysis of the rhetoric and dialogic elements of the poem demonstrate its brilliant lyrical, social, and thematic character. Newsom concludes by stating that the dialogical relationship between chapter 28 and what precedes is not easy enough to engage. She does, however, argue that one can "trace dotted lines that links [sic] this chapter with Job's final speech in chapters 29–31" (2003, 181).

I believe, however, that Job 28 is the narrator's radical but formal introduction to the process of Wisdom therapy developed in the part II of the book of Job. The basic Wisdom therapy process begins with an understanding of the importance, locus, and science of Wisdom. As a member of the Wisdom School, the narrator appropriates an ancient poem on the way to locate Wisdom as a key stage of the therapy process. The fundamental question is "where can Wisdom be found and who can find it?" (28:12).

In my volume entitled, *Discerning Wisdom in God's Creation: Following the Way of Ancient Scientists*, I outline the features of the ancient Wisdom School, its thinking, techniques, and traditions (Habel 2015, ch. 1). The wise were a discrete part of the community, distinct from the priests, prophets, royalty, and other sectors in society.

Among the various techniques that were typical of the *modus operandi* of the wise in ancient Israel were their "scientific" approaches to nature. The task of the wise "scientist" was to "observe" (*ra'a*) domains of nature and to "discern" (*bin*) their basic character or "way" (*derek*) and their "place" (*maqom*) in the design of nature. In this context, it is important to recognize that for the wise scientist, Wisdom was not first and foremost something humans "acquired" (*qana*), but

> *A driving force in nature, a dynamic dimension of the universe discerned by ancient scientists of the Wisdom School, a force that warrants investigation even today.* (Habel 2015, 11)

Wisdom in this school of thought was not primarily a depth of knowledge acquired by the wise, but a vibrant innate force or dimension in the domains of nature, and ultimately in the cosmos (cf. Habel 2021).

Job's friends were would-be therapists who claimed to know about Wisdom. Zophar, for example, claims to know not only about mercy and justice but also about the inherent Wisdom of God. For Zophar, God's Wisdom is inscrutable, but Job's situation is obvious; he has obviously committed some terrible crime to deserve the losses he has suffered.

> *Oh, if only God would speak*
> *and talk to you himself,*
> *he would expand the secrets of Wisdom,*
> *for there are two sides to understanding.*
> *Know that God exacts from you*
> *less than your guilt demands.* (11:5–6)

Ironically, the God who finds Wisdom does finally speak, but his therapy does not focus directly on the personal guilt or trauma of Job but beyond Job on the Wisdom design of the cosmos.

Job, too, was familiar with the Wisdom tradition but found it frustrating. He sarcastically asserts that Wisdom will die with his friends, but if they were silent that would count as Wisdom for them (12:2; 13:3).

Job, in the midst of his trauma, associates God's inherent Wisdom with his power and declares,

> *With him are Wisdom and power,*
> *his are counsel and understanding.*
> *When he breaks down there is no rebuilding,*
> *when he imprisons there is no release,*
> *when he holds back, the waters they dry up,*
> *when he lets them loose, they overthrow the earth.*
> (12:13–15)

In Job 28, however, the misunderstanding of divine Wisdom reflected in the speeches of the friends and of Job himself is exposed when the narrator outlines an account of how God, the supreme Wisdom Scientist, demonstrates the basic skills of a genuine Wisdom Scientist, researches all realms across the face of Earth, and locates the "place" in the domains of nature where Wisdom is to be found.

In Job 28, the narrator introduces the process of Wisdom therapy not only by introducing a crucial dimension of Wisdom but also by introducing a God who is a Wisdom Scientist, who knows both the nature and locus of Wisdom. It is this cosmic presence of Wisdom that Job is about to experience through the voice of a Wisdom therapist.

One can hardly imagine the shock of the traumatized Wisdom community in Canaan when the narrator takes them back to school and confronts them with an ancient Wisdom tradition that is in radical conflict not only with the teachings of the covenant theology that the postexilic Israelite community endorsed but also with the limited popular views of Wisdom as accumulated knowledge from the elders and accepted popular images of the inherent Wisdom of God.

After empathizing with his Wisdom community as he traced their anguish through the lengthy trauma experiences of Job, the narrator breaks the pattern of his relationship and resurrects an understanding of their Wisdom God that is radical and liberating. Wisdom is not to be discerned by trying to understand the mind of God but by recognizing that Wisdom is a cosmic reality that God has observed, discerned, and celebrated.

The narrator introduces God, the Wisdom Scientist, the Creator who discerns Wisdom in his creation (not in his head), a perspective that must have challenged his community and forced them to probe their past perspective about their God as a God with inherent Wisdom.

Because this interpretation of Wisdom by the narrator is so confronting and challenging for the Wisdom community, I believe it is valid to name it "The Wisdom Manifesto."

It is significant that the Wisdom therapy that the divine therapist employs in this context is radically different from the Wisdom therapy that is associated with bodies such as the contemporary Wisdom Therapy Institute. In these current contexts, Wisdom therapy is understood to be a comprehensive, scientifically established, practical approach to the challenges and conflicts in life.

Wisdom is understood to include profound personal and social skills developed over the years. Wisdom therapy involves,

Cognitive behavioural therapy, mindfulness meditation and the active cultivation of humility (www.wisdomtherapy. com).

While some components of contemporary Wisdom therapy may include developing an awareness of the person's relationship with the big picture and the domains of nature, the focus is primarily on gaining an inner Wisdom that will enable the sufferer to find personal healing.

The Wisdom therapy outlined below, however, reflects a radically different orientation and technique to most contemporary approaches.

Another significant type of recent trauma therapy involves "the healing of memories." Sufferers keep retelling their stories until they "find a new meaning in them and they start in earnest the work of healing" (West 2015, 224).

In the Wisdom therapy employed by the God of the narrator of the book of Job, however, Job does not rehearse all the pains of his life again, even though Job outlines his personal history in his litigation narrative. In this Wisdom therapy, Job is taken on a journey with a different God—this God's own life story is related to the cosmos and its origins. On that journey, Job experiences the therapy of endless questions about the wonders and design of a Wisdom-filled universe.

The outcome of this form of Wisdom therapy is for Job to gain an amazing cosmic consciousness, a profound Wisdom consciousness, and a challenging primordial consciousness—a new relationship with the Wisdom presence in the cosmos that surrounds him and the enigma of a God, the Wisdom Scientist who discerned Wisdom in creation.

Everything Precious Has Its Place!

The discourse in Job 28 assumes that Wisdom is the most precious commodity to be found on the face of the Earth. Moreover, according to ancient Wisdom thinking, every precious commodity—whether it be valuable metals, silver, gold or precious gems—has its designated locus or "place" in the natural world.

Human miners probe the depth of mountains and hills to locate the place of these precious commodities, even if that entails a dangerous investigation. Humans will risk their lives to locate the "place" of the precious in hidden locations (vv. 1–11).

But Where Is the Hidden "Place" of Wisdom?

Then the narrator poses the ultimate question for the scientist of the day:

> But Wisdom, where can she be found?
> Where is the "place" of Discernment? (28:12)

Wisdom is the most precious component of the cosmos— hidden, it seems, even from Death and the forces of the underworld.

It is more precious than all the gems and stones that humans may be able to discover. Wisdom is the most precious dimension of existence, the goal of all who seek meaning or answers to the deep questions of life. The question remains: How can Wisdom, the most precious find of all, be discovered?

The narrator repeats the crucial question by asking,

> But Wisdom where does she originate?
> Where is the "place" of Discernment? (28:20)

An answer, that Job's friends and others may assume, is that Wisdom is with God, in the mind of God, hidden from the eyes of the living (vv. 21–22).

God Did the Research of a Wisdom Scientist

The radical surprise revealed in this manifesto is that God is the one who first searched and found Wisdom. God is portrayed as the supreme Sage, the expert Wisdom Scientist, the model for those who seek Wisdom. God is the Wisdom expert, not because of the Wisdom inherent in God but because God had the skills necessary to discover and discern Wisdom.

> God "discerned" her way (derek),
> and came to know her place (maqom),
> for God looked to the ends of Earth
> and "observed" (ra'a) everything under heaven.
>   (28:23–24)

God, the supreme Sage, discerns the "way" (*derek*), the innate character of Wisdom, and the *maqom*, the designated "place" of Wisdom, by searching to the ends of Earth, by "observing" (*ra'a*) everything under the heavens.

Wisdom is a reality located on/in Earth, a reality that God, the Wisdom expert, has located by observing with the skills of a true Wisdom Scientist, the skills required of every Wisdom seeker.

God "observes" everything! Observing is the research technique that every wise person was expected to practice in order to "discern" the way of Wisdom in nature (e.g., Prov 6:6). And where does God discern Wisdom? In the "weight of the wind," in the "rule of the rain," and in the "way" of the thunderstorm (28:25–27).

Wisdom is not simply in the thunderstorm but is identified as its "way" (*derek*), its innate nature, its inner character and unique identity (Habel 2014, 12).

Wisdom is not simply in the rain, but in that "law" of nature that governs the rain as well as the other forces of nature.

In the culture of the First Nations peoples of Australia, God "reads the landscape" and in so doing "sees" and "discerns" the truth about the truth/law/Wisdom of the land.

I have often wondered why, at this point in the book of Job, the narrator inserted this portrait of God as the model Wise One, the ancient scientist who was able to observe nature and discern Wisdom. The main reason, I now believe, is to prepare the traumatized Wisdom community for the dramatic introduction of God as the Wisdom therapist in chapter 38.

The God who knows how to discern Wisdom becomes the therapist who can challenge Job to follow a similar path and discern the cosmic design, the Wisdom blueprint of the universe.

God, however, not only discovers Wisdom but also embraces Wisdom and makes it part of the world. First, God sees (*ra'a*) it again; that is, he now observes it as a discrete entity, an entity he saw when he searched the ends of the Earth (v. 24).

Next, God "appraises" and "establishes" Wisdom. It is recognized by God as the governing principle of the universe, the blueprint of the cosmos. In Proverbs 8, God is said to have acquired (*qana*) Wisdom, which becomes the blueprint involved in the design of the cosmos. Job 28 suggests one skillful way in which God the scientist/creator "acquired" Wisdom in the process of creation.

Finally, God "probes" Wisdom to test its value and character, just as humans "probe/penetrate" the depths of Earth to find precious metals and gems (v. 3).

God not only acquires Wisdom but also establishes it in creation and activates it in his role as a divine Sage.

The postscript that is added in verse 28 has been variously interpreted. It may be viewed as a later addition by the pious faithful in the Wisdom School who espoused another tradition, namely that Wisdom is gained by due reverence for their God. That viewpoint would be consistent with the theology of the friends.

Another explanation is to view this as a challenge for humans who would be wise to follow the methodology of God the Wisdom Scientist and observe the domains of nature so that they, like God, may discover Wisdom. If so, we may well designate the postscript as a sarcastic punch line!

Truths of The Wisdom Manifesto

1. Wisdom, though hidden, is the most valuable commodity on Earth, more valuable than gold, silver, or precious gems located within the Earth.
2. Wisdom was first discovered by God, who as a primordial Wisdom Scientist located Wisdom by employing the techniques of Wisdom science during the time of creation.
3. Wisdom can be located by employing the same techniques of Wisdom science, searching across the face of

Earth, reading the landscape, "observing" nature, and "discerning" the locus of Wisdom in creation.

4. Wisdom is a vibrant innate force in the various domains of nature, discerned, tested, and established by God, the original Wisdom Scientist, as a driving force in the design and function of creation.

5. Cosmic Wisdom is ultimately more important to discern than God if the sufferer is to discover the meaning of life as an active component of their cosmos.

CHAPTER 18

Job's Legislation Case that Precedes His Wisdom Therapy

Job 31

> *The resilience*
> *of the trauma sufferer may*
> *reach a point where there is*
> *a forceful innate drive*
> *to record the painful details*
> *of the trauma experience narrative*
> *under oath.*

JOB CHAPTERS 28–31 may be identified as the climax of Job's discourses and explorations. After numerous attempts to imagine taking God to court, Job only experienced additional trauma and angst. On one occasion he screamed in frustration,

> *Of course, I know this is so:*
> *a mortal cannot win a suit against El.*
> *If one chooses to bring him to trial*
> *he would not answer one charge in a thousand.*
> *He is wise of heart and mighty in power:*
> *who then can challenge him and emerge whole?*
> (9:2–4)

Nevertheless, his impulse to confront God with his innocence, in the face of apparent divine retribution, persisted. His trauma

also persists, however, because he believes God will terrify him in
court as he has during his recent life. Again, he cries,

> *Only grant me, El, two things,*
> *so I need not hide from your face.*
> *Keep your hand distant from me*
> *and let your terror not intimidate me.*
> *You summon me and I will be respondent,*
> *or I will state my case and you refute me.*
> *How many are my iniquities and sins?*
> *Inform me of my transgression and sin.* (13:20–23)

Job even has a wild dream that Earth will hear the cry of his
innocent blood and that a witness in heaven will hear her response
so that his innocence might be recognized.

> *O Earth, cover not my blood*
> *and let my cry have no place.*
> *Surely my witness is in heaven,*
> *he who can testify for me on high.*
> *Let him be my advocate, my friend before Eloah,*
> *when my eye weeps in his presence.*
> *Let him mediate between a mortal and Eloah*
> *as between one human being and another.*
> (16:18–21)

The wild dream of taking God to court so that his divine
adversary may face the truth and declare Job innocent is a pivotal
hope that only intensifies Job's trauma. The dream seems impossible and the obstacles seem beyond the capacity of a human to
overcome. God stands as the immovable adversary and the overpowering opponent.

In Job 29–31, however, Job takes a leap of faith into the abyss of the impossible and prepares his case for litigation against God, regardless of the consequences. The literary context for his case is presented in three parts, a) a narrative account of when he was blessed, held in honor by his community, known for administering justice and recognized as one of the wise whose voice was to be heeded (ch. 29), b) the story of how those in the community who treated him unfairly have assaulted him and have abused him, denying him any measure of justice (ch. 30), c) a litigation with a series of oaths relating to how he has conducted his behavior as a righteous citizen who deserves justice (ch. 31).

In terms of the therapy process, chapter 31 represents the final submission of Job's litigation case, a series of scripts that bear his signature. Job even calls for his divine adversary at law to submit a similar written declaration. With supreme irony, Job declares that if his adversary does submit such a document, Job will wear it like a crown.

The Wisdom narrator prepares the way for the advent of Wisdom therapy for his traumatized Wisdom community by having Job emerge from his trauma ordeals and make a bold public statement that records the basic story of his life of righteousness and empathy, a life that deserves none of the unwarranted cruelty he has experienced. Job's actions are a challenge for the suppressed voice of the Wisdom community to be made public.

Job's Public Declaration of Integrity

This text is the script for Job's public litigation, his declaration of innocence formulated in a series of oaths that would presumably be considered valid and appropriate for a court case on Earth in Job's day. The dilemma Job faces, however, is that his adversary at

law is considered a celestial being and the location of a trial with
such an adversary remains complicated.

After an initial declaration that he has never let his eyes be
seduced by a virgin, Job introduces the primary focus of the case:
the doctrine of divine reward and retribution. According to that
teaching, a fixed destiny or "fate" is apportioned for all areas
of the cosmos, including the wicked. Job had expected, therefore,
that his righteous life would be rewarded with blessings. But his
experience at God's hands led him to challenge the doctrine he
once espoused (vv. 1–4).

In verses 5–6, Job resumes the themes of his earlier oath of
integrity (27:4–6). Deceit and dissimulation are alien to Job's
character; he is a model of righteousness and integrity (cf. 27:5–6).
Accordingly, he is willing to be weighed in God's eternal scales of
justice to verify his claim (vv. 5–6).

Job's Oaths of Integrity

Job's first sequence of oaths are declarations that support his
integrity as a righteous man. He claims that his eyes have never
led him astray and caused him to commit a wrong (vv. 7–8). He
denies ever having committed adultery with any of woman in his
neighborhood, acutely aware that such an action is a "criminal
offense" (vv. 9–12).

Job also declares that he has never been guilty of avarice,
acquiring riches to satisfy his greed. He has never desired wealth
or glory (vv. 24–28). Nor has he ever been vindictive, rejoicing at
his enemy's ruin or celebrating his downfall (vv. 29–31).

Job's Oaths of Empathy

Job's case is not based entirely on his avoidance of acts of adultery
and evil. He has been a humane human who has had empathy for

all his servants. He even listened when they had a complaint. He is nonplussed, therefore, that his God might cross-examine Job in court as if he has been a cruel master (vv. 13–15).

Job's oaths of empathy extend to the poor, the widow, the orphan, and those devoid of clothing. These recipients of his goodness responded with blessings. Job declares that if he has ever lacked compassion, he should expect a calamity from his God. But he declares himself innocent of any lack of empathy (vv. 16–23).

Job goes so far as to highlight his hospitality, declaring that no stranger ever spent the night on the street. Job welcomed any traveler, regardless of the danger it might have involved. Job was hospitable even if his neighbors scorned his generosity (vv. 32–34).

Job's Closing Bravado

Job closes his declaration of innocence with three bold exclamations: 1) Time for someone, whether earthly or celestial, to come forward and be the judge who hears his case, since God, who is traditionally understood to be the judge, is now the adversary; 2) Job has not only made a series of unequivocal oaths, but he is also ready to add his signature to make his testimony a legal document; 3) Job calls on God, his adversary, to become a legal respondent and draft a comparable document outlining God's case as defendant.

In addition, with a measure of unexpected bravado, Job declares that if God, his legal respondent, did dare to draft a document, Job would convert the document into a crown and would boldly wear it on his head, prancing around as if he were a prince.

He concludes by declaring that just as he earlier hoped that the Earth would cry out because his innocent blood had been shed, he would now expect the ground of Earth to cry out against him if any of his testimony was untrue (vv. 38–40).

In the face of his final confrontation with God, his adversary in litigation, Job is unequivocal in his demand for justice.

Upon further reflection, the Wisdom narrator's portrayal of Job taking a manuscript on which the words of God are written and folding it into a crown to wear without shame is tantamount to a comic closure. The case against the Covenant God is over and in the end amounts to a humorous finale, the close of a long and onerous experience.

CHAPTER 19

Elihu, the Would-Be Wisdom Arbiter

Job 32

In religious contexts,
a trauma sufferer
may experience the presumptuous counseling
of young would-be therapists
who claim to represent God
and possess the Wisdom
to provide counsel for the sufferer,
counsel that needs to be rejected as
a futile stage
in the healing process.

IN CHAPTERS 28–31, Job prepared documents that are the written litigation script he is ready to present before his God in a court of law. His documents represent a significant leap of faith in his Wisdom journey of healing, a bold possibility of moving beyond the domain of his horrendous trauma to a moment of dramatic confrontation and resolution.

Instead of God appearing immediately in response to Job's challenging declaration of innocence, however, we are faced with another bold individual who claims to possess the Wisdom required to be an arbiter and resolve Job's case of litigation. All the prior claims of Job and the responses of the three friends in previous chapters are dismissed by a young "sage" who proceeds to present an alternative Wisdom perspective that will solve Job's trauma dilemmas.

As a would-be Wisdom arbiter, Elihu does not reflect any empathy for Job's trauma and angst. Instead, he claims to have the Wisdom to unveil the truth relating to Job's condition. As a would-be arbiter, Elihu assumes he has the capacity to stand between Job and God in an earthly arbitration. As a would-be arbiter, Elihu claims the right to represent God in the arbitration envisioned by Job.

The plan of the narrator to lead his Wisdom community with Job on a tour of the cosmos with the divine Wisdom therapist is interrupted. A young member of the community is bold enough to halt the therapy process being used by the narrator. This young member of the Wisdom community claims that he has the Wisdom necessary to solve Job's problem and heal his trauma.

Instead of expecting their Wisdom God to handle the pains of the traumatized Wisdom community, this young sage claims to possess incarnate Wisdom. In fact, he asserts that everyone in the community possesses innate Wisdom and should know how to counsel Job successfully.

And the source of that innate Wisdom? The very breath of God that animates all humans! In the mind of Elihu, there is no need for the narrator to proceed any further. The Wisdom of Elihu is sufficient! He has the breath/spirit of God.

Introducing Elihu

Rather unexpectedly, the Wisdom narrator provides more details to introduce Elihu than he does for the three friends of Job. Elihu is identified as a bright young man from a known background who has waited patiently before commencing his lengthy speeches. While the narrator portrays Elihu as an angry youth who is distraught because he finds Job claiming to be more righteous than God, his actual speeches reflect a stable set of arguments that suggest the calm and considered stance of a would-be arbiter representing his God.

The narrator contends that Elihu is upset because Job has made God appear to be the guilty party, a position this righteous young man cannot tolerate. Yet the speeches he presents are more than an angry outburst of a hotheaded youth. They are a series of options that Job ought to consider to enable healing and harmony. Elihu represents a reasonable position to take charge of Job's case himself.

Incarnate Wisdom

I have written elsewhere about innate Wisdom or Wisdom as an incarnate life force (Habel 2015, ch. 2). The significance of Elihu's claim is not only that he possesses innate Wisdom but also that his incarnate Wisdom, even though located in a young man, is superior to that of his elders who traditionally believe that Wisdom comes with age.

It is significant in the Wisdom orientation of the book of Job, that contrary to the focus on Wisdom located in the forces of nature in Job 28, Elihu maintains the tradition that Wisdom and insight are present in humans precisely because all humans are animated by the very breath of God that animated Adam. His stance is contrary to the claims of Eliphaz, Bildad, and Job about the nature of Wisdom (Habel 2021, ch. 3).

The Hebrew *ruach hi'* in verse 8 may be rendered "her spirit" or "she is the spirit," the "she" referring back to Wisdom. Elihu claims that the animating "spirit of God" within a person is the source of Wisdom, or indeed one with Wisdom. For Elihu, the "life-giving spirit" and "Wisdom-imparting spirit" are one and justify Elihu claiming to be an arbiter who understands the arbitration process better than the aged who are no longer wise.

The Absence of an Arbiter

Elihu's compulsion to be an arbiter is grounded, in part, by his contention that, despite all the arguments pronounced by Job's friends, there is no arbiter in Job's litigation case. While the term *arbiter* may refer to a mediator who is ready to hear both sides of the argument and offer a resolution, in this context Elihu claims to have heard all the arguments delivered by Job and his friends.

Elihu is now ready to speak as God's advocate to enable a Wisdom resolution that is superior to the alleged Wisdom of the friends who say, "Let El, not humans, refute Job."

Earlier, Job had sought someone to arbitrate his case openly and fairly (9:33; 16:21). Finally, he called for a court case in which an arbiter would preside and hear Job's case (31:35). Now, Elihu steps up to be the arbiter, the final voice before the envisioned court of justice.

A Compulsion to Speak

Elihu here makes a public announcement that he plays his role as arbiter and counters Job's arguments by speaking his mind as a young man animated by Wisdom. The irony of Elihu's announcement is evident in verse 18 where he claims that his belly is full of wind. Earlier in verse 8 he claimed that all humans possess incarnate Wisdom, for all possess the "spirit" (*ruach*) within them.

When he again describes his own inner spirit, he employs terms reflected in the satirical language used by Eliphaz (15:2). Elihu inadvertently describes himself as a windbag, a man with "wind" bloating his belly. Elihu's portrayal of himself may reflect the subtle manipulation of the tradition by the narrator. Even so, Elihu's innate Wisdom is a forceful factor that Job and the reader are challenged to consider as a stage in the healing process.

While many scholars have dismissed Elihu's opening speech as the irrelevant words of a boasting teenager, I would argue that he highlights an alternative Wisdom tradition. In the introduction to this volume, I identified four major Wisdom traditions: inherent divine Wisdom, accumulated human Wisdom, acquired Wisdom, and Wisdom innate in nature.

In the mind of the narrator, it would seem, Elihu's vision of God is a satire that is rendered sheer folly by the Wisdom God who takes Job on a tour of the cosmos in the following chapters where Wisdom is discerned as a cosmic presence—not just a thunderstorm of El.

CHAPTER 20

The Wisdom Therapist Stirs Job's Cosmic Consciousness

Job 38

> *Wisdom therapy*
> *involves responding to a range of*
> *insightful questions that enable you to leap*
> *from the misery of the moment*
> *into the mysteries of the cosmos,*
> *from the turmoil of trauma*
> *into the unknown of the universe,*
> *where Wisdom is a pervasive,*
> *positive presence*
> *and its role*
> *a therapeutic force*
> *that binds*
> *and guides the realms*
> *of creation.*

CHAPTER 38 IS a brilliant poetic discourse reflecting a subtle but significant series of penetrating questions that are tantamount to an ancient expression of Wisdom therapy. The God of this therapy is the Wisdom Scientist of Job 28, a radically different deity from the thunderous God of righteousness defended by Elihu in the preceding chapters.

In my commentary on Job (1985), I designated this chapter "Yahweh's Defence of his Cosmic Order," assuming this chapter represented a divine response to the insinuations of Job about his God's operations on Earth, found in his earlier speeches.

Reading from a trauma perspective, I now realize that in these chapters, God is portrayed by the Wisdom narrator as challenging Job to follow the techniques of searching for Wisdom found in Job 28. The God who is hailed as the successful Wisdom Scientist in Job 28 is here summoning Job to follow the same *modus operandi* to discern Wisdom by "looking to the ends of Earth and observing/seeing everything under the sky" (28:23–24). Job is challenged to "read" the cosmic landscape!

I would now argue that: The Wisdom narrator depicts this God as a Wisdom Therapist challenging Job to become a Wisdom Scientist, not a screaming victim.

A subtle technique of the narrator in this divine discourse is to treat Job as if he were a primordial figure like Wisdom itself (as in Proverbs 8). This ironic device is evident when God says, for example, "Surely you know, for you were born then" (v. 21). Whatever the mythical memory associated with this literary device, the text locates Job beside a Creator God who discerns Wisdom at the core of the process of creation (28:23–27). Job is challenged to research the primordial and discern Wisdom in the way that God, the original Wisdom Scientist (of Job 28), operated during the process of creation.

The Wisdom orientation of this discourse is also apparent from the range of technical Wisdom School terms embedded in the text, terms such as *way, place, discern/ment, Wisdom, see/observe, design,* and *law* (Habel 2015, ch. 1).

In the Wisdom Therapy employed by this God of Job, Job is not required to rehearse his life, even though he had outlined his history in his litigation speech. In God's Wisdom therapy, Job is taken on a journey with this God—God's life story relating to the cosmos—to enable Job to experience a bold cosmic consciousness in the primordial.

The God YHWH that the Wisdom narrator claims is the voice from the whirlwind is clearly not the divine caricature called YHWH found in the prologue NOR the Covenant God of the friends OR the storm God El that Elihu claims to defend. The new YHWH seems to be one with the Wisdom Scientist of the Wisdom Manifesto, despite the sarcastic postscript at the end of Job 28. Unless, of course, the name YHWH was also added to the text at the beginning of Job 38 so that later editors could justify including Job in the canon.

It is a common feature of trauma readings of biblical texts that the interpreter seeks to recognize how the suffering of the community is often hidden, or in the case of the book of Job, how a narrator uses a legendary figure such as Job to portray the depths of the anguish and despair of the community involved. It is somewhat of a surprise to encounter the healing process involved in such a community, a process that I have identified as Wisdom therapy in the case of the traumatized Wisdom community that Job represents.

The narrator, it would seem, is not only bold enough to confront his community with the traditional image of their Wisdom God as the original scientist who discerned Wisdom as a force innate in creation (Job 28), but also dares to reveal the "Wisdom mentor cum therapist" who challenges his community to leap from their moment of misery into the Wisdom mysteries alive in the realms of the cosmos.

If members of the Wisdom community are willing to identify with Job, they take the risk of traveling back in time to the primordial, intrigued by the amazing design of the cosmos and encountering Wisdom innate in the operation of the diverse worlds of time and space. In short, they are destined to acquire a cosmic Wisdom consciousness that changes their entire understanding of God and their relationship with the world around them.

According to the Wisdom narrator of the book of Job, the wise human being called Job experienced the tragic loss of all his property and all his children, deep despair in the face of a life without meaning, a cruel trauma that he believed was inflicted by God, and counsel from his friends that he deserved divine retribution.

Job also experienced a readiness to accuse God of unjust punishment and pain, a bold impulse to take God to court to prove Job's innocence, pretrial trauma when he anticipated fierce divine intervention, and the courage to draft a written declaration for his court case.

And then, Job experiences the shock of a "whirlwind" that may well be designated "shock therapy," or at least a shock that initiates therapy.

While the voice from the whirlwind may appear to reflect a common theophanic tradition, the process is one of discerning interrogation, not revelation of divine truths or messages. The image of the Wisdom Therapist is radically different from the images of the Covenant God in the discourses of the friends. The task of Job is to explore mysteries in a complex cosmos, not to heed a revelation from the traditional God of Israel.

The Shock

According to the narrator,

> *Then YHWH answered Job from the whirlwind and said,*
> *"Who is this who clouds my design in darkness,*
> *presenting arguments without knowledge?*

> *Gird up your loins like a hero.*
> *I will ask questions and you will inform me."*
>   (vv. 1–3)

There are, I would contend, three dimensions to the shock intervention of this God into Job's miserable life, at this point in time:

a.   The Whirlwind *(se'ara)*

The "whirlwind" that intervenes is not just a strong wind. The term *se'ara* refers to a severe storm or tempest, like the storm that comes out of the North when Ezekiel has his vision (Ezek 1:4). In the fierce storm that confronts Job, God seems to be audibly present in a manner that would shock the daylights out of a human.

That is precisely what Job feared earlier in one of his traumatic episodes. He exclaimed that if God did appear,

> *He would crush me with a "whirlwind,"*
> *and increase my wounds without cause.* (9:17)

Clearly the "whirlwind" is not a friendly wind gliding over his face like the one Eliphaz claimed to have experienced (4:15). A whirlwind is a storm that normally crushes and leaves the object of the experience stunned, shocked, and helpless.

Moreover, the "answer" from such a whirlwind is not a gentle breeze. For Elijah, God was not in the "great strong wind that rent the mountains" but is "a still small voice" (1 Kings 11:12). For Job, the answer of God is the opposite, a challenge from within a great strong storm, an ancient form of "shock therapy," not typical of the Wisdom tradition.

b. The Challenge

The response of YHWH does not express any sympathy for the suffering and despair Job has experienced. Nor does the response express any dismay or anger at the numerous accusations that Job made about the way God has treated him as an innocent human being. Nor is there any reference at this point to the litigation claims made by Job if God dared to confront him in court.

The challenge of this God is readily understood by some scholars to be an accusation that Job has obscured the design of God by his repeated charges (9:5–13; 10:8–14; 12:13–25). The challenge, however, may also be interpreted as a clue regarding the therapy Job will experience, namely an understanding of "my design."

Pivotal for an understanding of this challenge is an appreciation of the term "design" (`etsa). This term is often parallel with the term for "Wisdom" (chokma) as in Proverbs 8:14 and 21:30. Earlier Job has declared,

> *With him are Wisdom and power,*
> *his are "design" and understanding.* (12:13)

As I have outlined in a number of my writings, Wisdom is not primarily an attribute of God in the Wisdom School of thought, but an innate force in nature (Job 28:23–27) and in some contexts tantamount to the "blueprint" for creation (Prov 8:22–23), the "design" for the cosmos.

> *In the Wisdom School, Wisdom exists as a primordial factor that precedes creation, a primal capacity whose nature and function is evident in Proverbs 8.* (Habel 2015, 39)

Job is first accused of hiding this great cosmic mystery called Wisdom and design, but then is challenged to be ready to answer the ultimate questions about this design, the very nature of the cosmos. Exploring the Wisdom innate in the cosmos is the potential therapy for Job that God announces.

c. Be a Geber

The third dimension of Job's shock therapy is the challenge for Job to be a *geber*, a strong man, or as sometimes translated "a hero." Job is no longer to sit on a pile of dust and ashes lamenting his lot as an innocent victim. Job must dismiss his traumas, gird his loins, and face the music—or more specifically, questions about the nature of the cosmos. The challenge to this "hero" is not one of strength but of knowledge, Wisdom, and discernment.

The irony in the wording of YHWH's challenge is the use of the word "know" in place of "answer" in verse 3b. Job had promised to answer if summoned (13:22). YHWH shocks Job by demanding more—that Job impart his expert knowledge to his apparently uninformed God.

Job's therapy begins after he experiences the shock of a terrifying storm that revealed this God's presence, a satirical challenge for Job to reveal his "superior" knowledge about the design of the cosmos and a closing charge to "pull up his pants," get rid of his winging, and take a journey through the cosmos as a potential Wisdom scientist together with a Wisdom Scientist called God.

Discern the Origins of Earth

The first set of therapeutic questions relates to an ancient tradition about the origins of Earth, a tradition that differs radically from other traditions about the origins of Earth throughout the Hebrew Scriptures. The image of Earth being constructed like a public edifice serves to highlight a structure of Earth that embraces a careful design, one such construction in the "design" of the cosmos that Job is to explore as a Wisdom scientist and to discern its character.

In addition, the completion of Earth's construction is viewed as a defining moment when the cornerstone is laid and the heavenly beings celebrate. Job is not only to discern the design of Earth itself but also to discern that he is privileged to live in a splendid domain worthy of cosmic celebration. This magnificent moment in creation stands in contradiction to Job's claim that God overthrows the structures of Earth (9:5–7).

Observe the "Limits" of the Ocean

The second vignette of questions focuses on the confinement of the chaos waters of the Sea to protect the newly constructed Earth. The Sea is personified as a primordial chaos monster whom God had to bring under control during the creation process in much the same way that the Canaanite God Baal had to control Yam (Sea) to win kingship and control chaos.

In the satirical language of this text, the chaos waters are reduced to a baby, born from a womb, placed in a playpen and told to stay in place.

The reference to hedging in waters of Sea may also have mythological roots, but in this context "hedging" may also be an allusion to Job's claim that God's hedging extends to the hedging of Job's "way/purpose" in life (3:23). Job also accused God of placing a muzzle on him as if he were the chaos waters of Sea (7:12).

The motif of limit is also significant. The "limit" refers to the order imposed on chaos at the beginning of creation and maintained for the protection of Earth (Ps 104:9). The limit is explicitly a "law" (*choq*, cf. Prov 8:29), thereby highlighting its character as an innate governing force in the cosmos. This discernment of a law that governs the ocean recalls the innate law that God, the Wisdom Scientist, discerned in the rain (28:26).

While the Wisdom narrator may not investigate the origins of chaos and its aftermath in creation, Job is challenged to discern the laws/limits that control chaos in the real world.

Locate the "Place" of Dawn

According to the Wisdom thinking of Job 28, every component of creation—even Wisdom—has its designated locus or "place" in the order of the universe. Job is challenged by the Wisdom Therapist to indicate where "Morning" and "Dawn" are located in the design of the cosmos, their designated place in the universe.

The language of this challenge may reflect the ancient Canaanite mythology of Ugarit where "Morning" and "Dawn" seem to be personified beings. Here Job is challenged to wake Dawn, whom he previously sought to restrain forever by imposing a curse on the night of his birth (3:7–9). Job is thereby challenged to discern the ordering principle of Wisdom that established the place for each component in the design of the cosmos.

The regulation of day and night was viewed as essential to the maintenance of cosmic order. Control of wickedness, which persists in creation, is not achieved by direct acts of divine intervention by a celestial deity or the Covenant God, but by the interplay of the forces of nature guided by Wisdom.

Probe the Domains of the Deep

In one ancient biblical tradition, the Deep is the great primordial abyss that penetrates the nether regions of the Earth that were brought under control by God in the creation process (Gen 1:2, 6; 7:11).

The realm of Death was also understood to be located in the netherworld, the domain where the living eventually descend (Job 30:23). The mortal must pass through the so-called gates of the underworld to reach Death. By summoning Job to probe the gloomy realms of the underworld, God is challenging Job's earlier claims about Sheol as a desirable land of equals (3:16–19) and a potential refuge from God's anger (14:13–15), especially for those contemplating suicide.

By employing the technical Wisdom terms "see" (*ra'a*), "discern" (*bin*), and "reveal" (*gala*), God is also challenging Job to ascertain whether he can even employ his skills as a Wisdom scientist to probe the hidden domains of Death and the underworld in the cosmology of the ancient world.

Discern the "Place" of Light and Darkness

Light and darkness are identified here as discrete domains that have hidden abodes like the *locus* of Wisdom itself, beyond the realm of the mysterious (28:20–21). Each has its "place" and "way" is the primordial blueprint of the cosmos. To discern their locations, the Wisdom scientist would also need to learn cosmic geography.

By addressing Job as if he were the first human, God may be merely employing biting sarcasm. In the context of Wisdom therapy, however, this God seems to be challenging Job to play the role of a Wisdom scientist alongside the Creator and see the locus of these domains in the design of the cosmos.

Observe the Wisdom of the Weather

Verses 22–23 focus on the first of a series of mysteries associated with the skies and the weather. Job is challenged to "see/observe," as a true Wisdom scientist, the "places" of snow and hail in the skies. Snow and hail are viewed not only as forces of nature but also as arsenals in times of adversity (Deut 28:12; Jer 10:13). Hail may not only fall in times of extreme cold, but also be a weapon of holy war (Josh 10:11).

The thunderstorm (in vv. 26–27) may at first appear to be an uncontrolled meteorological happening. The use of the Wisdom term *way* in relation to both lightning and thunder, however, emphasizes that both of these weather phenomena are governed by innate forces of nature, just as rain is controlled by an innate "rule" (28:26).

The significance of the rainstorm here is the beneficial role it plays across the Earth, even in uninhabited wastelands. Thunderstorms are the source of a divine blessing for fields and forests, a blessing Job did not appreciate in the misery of his trauma.

The origins of ice and frost are likewise surrounded in mystery, as is the role they can play when gentle drops of rain may be transformed into sheets of ice that seem to hide the Deep.

Research the Realms of Space

Job is also led to observe the world of space, its constellations and laws. The narrator's knowledge of this cosmic domain may well surprise us even today.

> *Can you bind the fetters of the Pleiades,*
> *or loosen the reins of Orion?*
> *Can you lead out Mazzaroth in its season,*
> *or guide the Bear with her sons?*
> *Do you know the "laws" of the sky?*
> *Can you establish their order on the land?*
> (Job 38:31–33)

Job's initial challenge is to probe traditional knowledge of the constellations. It is one thing to observe and wonder at their design and pattern in the sky; it is quite another to contemplate how these constellations in space are controlled by a Wisdom that is beyond human ingenuity. The narrator views the skies as a domain filled with both mystery and mythology, the scientific and the spiritual.

Even more stunning, perhaps, is the question posed about the "laws" (*chuqoth*) of the skies (v. 33). The focus is clearly on Wisdom as an innate science, not on some deity who controls the heavens or manipulates the stars. We might even identify the laws in the skies governing the cosmos with contemporary understandings of gravity and related astral forces. Just as Wisdom is found by God in the "laws" of nature associated with the weather (28:25–26), Job is challenged to be a Wisdom scientist and discern the same Wisdom functioning in the laws of space.

God, the Wisdom Scientist, asks whether these laws can be employed to establish an ordered world on Earth: a genuine mystery of ancient or modern astrophysics. This question relates to the very core of ecology as a science.

How do the laws of one domain interrelate with those of another domain? How do the laws of space interact and affect the *modus operandi* of planet Earth? How do the laws of the cosmos relate to each other to facilitate the operation of the universe and the place of Earth in that universe? How does space function as a dimension of the cosmic design Job is challenged to "discern"?

In short, Job is confronted with one of the great mysteries of astrophysics, the cosmic ecology of time and space and the function of Wisdom in that ecology. Ultimately, Job is challenged to discern how his Earth relates to the realms of space rather than the gods of the heavens.

Investigate the Wisdom in the Clouds

The evidence that Wisdom is not, in the Wisdom School tradition, primarily a mature knowledge gleaned by humans over time is quite evident from the key verse in this text:

> *Who put Wisdom in the cloud canopy*
> *and who gave Discernment to my pavilion?* (v. 36)

This Wisdom located in the cloud canopy is to be distinguished from the Wisdom skills of Wisdom students who attempt to "count the clouds." The initial response of many readers is to assume that God placed Wisdom in the clouds. But, as the Wisdom science of Job 28 has revealed, Wisdom is an innate force of nature, including the clouds.

Wisdom is quite clearly an innate principle in each of the domains of the cosmos according to the primal design of the universe that Job has been invited to explore. Job has been challenged, at a dramatic stage in his Wisdom therapy, to move beyond the boundaries of his personal trauma tragedies to explore the mysteries of the cosmos that a Wisdom scientist may discern, and in so doing gain an alternative understanding of their world than the local tragedies of life may seem to suggest.

Of the many insights that may have emerged from this classic portrait of Wisdom in the book of Job, there are two that have changed my consciousness over the years.

The first is the profound recognition that in the design of the cosmos, however one may have once understood its origins, there exists a primordial blueprint called Wisdom that is the ultimate source of the numerous innate forces of nature that operate as principles that activate and sustain the universe in all its complexity and grandeur.

The second is a mode of therapy that transcends traditional approaches that dwell upon the personal pains of trauma and that challenges the sufferer to take a leap of faith into the world of wonders that reveal a mystery called Wisdom.

That mystery is an innate cosmic web of wonders to which all human beings belong, whatever their circumstance, a web of wonders that can have a healing effect for those willing to follow the journey of Job, embrace the permeating presence of Wisdom, and experience cosmic consciousness.

CHAPTER 21

The Wisdom Therapist Stirs Job's Wisdom Consciousness

Job 39

> *Wisdom therapy may also involve*
> *responding to a range of*
> *insightful questions*
> *that enable you to leap*
> *from the misery of the moment*
> *into the mysteries of Wisdom*
> *in the world*
> *of the wild.*

AFTER THE BRILLIANT poetic discourse challenging Job to discern Wisdom in the domains of the cosmos (Job 38), the Wisdom Therapist challenges Job to explore the world of the wild to discern its sapiential mysteries.

Significantly, the realms where Job is expected to discover the "answers" to the profound questions posed by the whirlwind therapist are in nature not society, in the domains of the cosmos and world of the wild, not the human communities where Job experienced his traumatic disasters.

The God whom Job encounters in the wild is far from the wild God that Job believed was harassing him in society, or the storm God El that Elihu claims to defend.

Job comes to know a God of cosmic Wisdom that transforms the trauma sufferer into a human being with a rich cosmic consciousness, an acute awareness of the domains of the cosmos to which he is connected by a common force called Wisdom.

The therapy session of chapters 38–39 is concluded with a closing challenge (40:1–5) for Job to answer the avalanche of questions posed by YHWH who previously summoned Job to "answer" (38:3). Job's response is not a confession of sin but a recognition of his limited knowledge about the God who has led him to discover Wisdom in the world at large.

Job does not confess; he concedes he has done no wrong but that his knowledge of God is limited!

The narrator of the traumatized Wisdom community, of which he has become a radical voice, moves the challenging questions of God from mysteries about the cosmos to insights about the wild. This Wisdom God is not just a presence who discerns Wisdom mysteries in the cosmos; this God can pose questions about the world of the wild with which members of the Wisdom community ought to be familiar. By exploring the operation of Wisdom among the creatures of the wild, the person experiencing trauma in society may experience a liberating vision in nature.

The World of the Wild

At first it may appear that challenging Job to demonstrate his capacity to participate in the domains of wild animals may be a strange form of therapy. A close analysis, from a trauma perspective, reveals that the Job who claims to be a victim of an arbitrary angry God may well be illuminated when he discovers the range of innate forces that God activates to sustain and celebrate the world of nature, of which humans are ultimately a crucial part.

These innate forces that characterize the creatures of the wild include the capacity of fierce animals like lions, or birds of prey like ravens, to find adequate food for their whelps and fledglings, the awareness of animals like ibex to deliver their young at the appropriate time and to care for them, the instinct of the wild ass to celebrate its home in the wilderness far from the shouts of a taskmaster, and the independence of the wild ox who cannot be tamed to serve human beings.

In addition, Job is confronted by the mystery of the ostrich who seems to lack the innate Wisdom needed to tend her young; the drive of the warhorse who exhibits extreme strength, fury, and exhilaration in the face of battle; and the discernment of the hawk and the eagle to live in the heights and yet find food for their young far below.

The Wisdom dimensions of this discourse are evident not only from the ironic claim that Eloah somehow forgot to endow the ostrich with the Wisdom necessary to rear her young but also in the range of innate capacities attested throughout nature. The ibex "know" their time of delivery. The hawk and the eagle have "the discernment" needed to soar over rocky crags. Every creature is expected to possess innate Wisdom, which is why the ostrich episode is so provocative. Innate Wisdom is tantamount to incarnate know-how!

By posing questions about the creatures of the wild, the therapist leads Job to move beyond his victim mentality as a traumatized human being to discern his "place" is the wider community of the wild where innate Wisdom guides all living creatures, even those in the wild, to celebrate life.

Job's Initial Response

Job's most famous response to the questions of the Wisdom Therapist is found in Job 42:1–6, where he declares that he has "seen you," whoever that may mean. In his initial response,

however, Job is reacting to the question of the new image of
YHWH,

> *Will the one with a suit against Shaddai correct*
> *me?*
> *Will the one arraigning Eloah answer me?* (v. 2)

Once again, God challenges Job to "answer" the powerful
questions of the preceding poem (cf. 38:2). Here, it seems, YHWH
acknowledges that Job is a hero (*geber*, 38:3) with a lawsuit against
Shaddai. YHWH, however, does not deal with the question of
Job's innocence or the issue of God's guilt. Instead, he challenges
Job to "correct" God's presentation of the mysteries of Wisdom
that characterize the "design" of the universe, assuming Job now
knows the answers as a Wisdom Scientist.

God acknowledges that Job is the one seeking to bring God to
court, but God responds by challenging Job to prove his capacity
to comprehend the ways of Wisdom in the cosmos rather than
face him in court.

In this response, Job recognizes he is "small," especially in the
context of the cosmic design. He does not confess "I have sinned"
or "I have done wrong." "I am small" implies "I am humbled by the
speeches of God just as I previously believed I was humbled by his
afflictions" (7:1–6). At this point, Job does not retract his case, but
neither does he renew his challenge against God. For Job the case
may be closed, but YHWH renews the challenge with the introduction of Behemoth and Leviathan in the speeches that follow.

A close reading of verse 9 is significant. The text reads: "Is the
wild ox willing to serve (*'abad*) you?" The implied answer to this
text undermines the famous mandate to dominate tradition in
Genesis 1:26–28, a tradition challenged by Job in his discourse
related to the *imago Dei* in chapter 7. In this text, God declares

that dominion over creatures such as the wild ass and the wild ox is not possible for humans. The wild ass defies the world of humans and refuses to obey a human taskmaster.

In the case of the wild ox, the verb "serve" is employed, a verb that is the diametric opposite of "rule" found in Genesis 1:28. It is not an integral part of the design of nature for wild things to be subjected to humans.

To add insult to injury, God describes just how ludicrous it would be were the wild ox to become Job's servant, babysitting beside his crib and harvesting all Job's grain. The wild ox is here portrayed as a docile lackey, completely untrue to its nature and its "way" as a creature of the wild.

CHAPTER 22

The Wisdom Therapist Stirs Job's Primordial Consciousness

Job 40–41

> *Exploring the primordial*
> *is one of the bizarre modes*
> *of Wisdom therapy,*
> *finding meaning in our origins*
> *rather than in the moment.*

THE FUNCTION OF Behemoth (ch. 40) and Leviathan (ch. 41) in the design of the book of Job has long been a subject of considerable debate. The key question is why the narrator includes these two figures in the classic speech of YHWH from the whirlwind. Several options may be considered.

The speech is based on iconographic evidence. Behemoth is identified with the red hippopotamus and Leviathan with the crocodile, or Behemoth and Leviathan are symbols of the mighty historical enemies of Israel (Ruprecht 1971, 209–231), mighty forces that YHWH controls.

Behemoth and Leviathan are mythic symbols of the forces of chaos that are overcome by Baal in the Canaanite traditions, by Marduk in the Babylonian Enuma Elish and by Horus in Egyptian mythology. Or Behemoth and Leviathan are mortal creatures like Job, didactic images employed by YHWH to teach Job about God's ways.

In my commentary of 1985, I wondered why the portrayal of these two extraordinary figures appears at the culmination of YHWH's speech: *Are they merely comic relief or do they focus the speech of YHWH to redirect Job's thinking in a specific way?* (1985, 558).

Now, in the context of a trauma hermeneutic and the closing Wisdom therapy employed by the divine Wisdom Scientist, the function of these two chapters is even more enigmatic.

I would now argue that the image of Behemoth is a creation of the narrator with a mysterious name that means "the beast." Behemoth is primordial, the symbol of the chaotic forces that God created at the beginning and that need to be kept subjugated. But the therapist does not just reflect on the past, he declares that Job is connected to the primordial, "made" at the same time as Behemoth.

One reaction would be to assume Job, created with Behemoth, is viewed as a comparable chaos monster, whom God must subdue. Or, in the language of the Wisdom School, Job is urged not only to "see/behold" the creatures of the wild that possess innate Wisdom and are part of God "design," but also to become aware that he, too, is connected with the primordial.

In this discourse, the therapist who has awakened Job's cosmic consciousness (ch. 38) and Job's Wisdom consciousness (ch. 39) now awakens Job's primordial consciousness. Job is also connected to the domains of chaos that are part of God's cosmic design.

The figure of Leviathan has mythological associations in Canaan and Israel. In Canaanite mythology, Baal is credited with having slain the serpent Leviathan:

> *When thou smotest Leviathan the slippery serpent*
> *and madest an end of the wriggling serpent,*
> *the tryant with seven heads.* (Baal III* i 1–3)

Likewise, YHWH is remembered for crushing the heads of Leviathan (Ps 74:12–14; cf. Isa 27:1). The mythic dimensions of this monster are also evident in the narrator's colorful portrayal of an invincible monster who "sneezes" flashes of lightning.

Earlier Job had accused his God of trying to muzzle Job, as if he were the primordial Sea, a threatening dragon monster (7:11–12). Now Job is taken by the Wisdom Therapist to behold Leviathan, another primordial chaos monster. No matter how terrifying the portrayal of this chaos monster may be, Job has been guided by the Wisdom Therapist to awaken his consciousness to the reality of the primordial that YHWH has kept under control as a domain of cosmic design.

The narrator of the traumatized Wisdom community now moves the challenging questions of God from mysteries about the cosmos to the "mystery" of the primordial. Control of chaos forces in the primordial is an amazing mystery that overshadows the trauma chaos in recent Israelite history or in the personal life of Job.

Job and his traumatized community are not just connected to the world of recent human history, with all its social and religious chaos, but also to the very origins of humanity and creation itself, a world born out of primordial chaos, a world governed by the presence of cosmic Wisdom.

More Challenging Questions

Once again, the Wisdom Therapist challenges Job to "answer" a series of questions in the process of dealing with Job's trauma, a God trauma evoked by the apparent injustice Job has experienced at the hands of his God.

The first question seems to deal with Job's claim that he is in the right and God is in the wrong. The following questions are provocative challenges, making fun of Job's claim to be righteous in the face of a righteous God. It is ridiculous for Job to assume he has the power of El and can thunder with a voice like his. That Job should challenge God's justice is here regarded by God as a joke.

And a Sarcastic Promise

This God not only laughs at the idea that Job could respond with a thunderous voice, God also enjoys a colorful satire in which he portrays Job as a mighty hero who can crush the wicked and debase the proud.

He then declares to the world that he, God, would pay homage to Job, the victorious hero—a ludicrous promise in a therapeutic context. Significant, however, is that this word from the whirlwind is not a word of judgment or an exposure of Job's guilt. Far from it! Job is still on the cosmic couch facing the need to understand his situation before a Wisdom-oriented God.

Behold Your Primordial Brother

When Behemoth is introduced, Job is called upon to do nothing but look, listen, and learn from his Wisdom Therapist. As in his earlier interrogation of Job in chapter 38, the therapist functions as the Wisdom Scientist and assumes Job is his companion in the primordial. Job is described as a primal creature made along with the mysterious Behemoth.

This is not a figure for Job to command like the eagle or control like the wild ox. Behemoth and Job are revealed to have a common origin; they are both primordial in a Wisdom-oriented way. In this insight from the therapist, the suffering human called Job is challenged to recognize that his origins reach back to the primordial, a world of primal creativity.

Behemoth is here introduced as Job's primordial brother.

Behemoth, the First of El's Ways

Behemoth, however, is more than Job's primordial brother. Behemoth is identified as the "first of El's way," an expression that is extremely significant.

The sense of the "first" in this context is clearly the primordial. In Proverbs 8:22, primordial Wisdom is the "way" that God acquires first, before his "works" of creation. How then can Behemoth be considered God's first "way"?

The answer, it seems, lies in the distinction the narrator makes between Wisdom as the primordial design that God acquires to create the cosmos and Behemoth as the first primordial creation according to that cosmic design. According to this tradition, it would seem, chaos was the first of God's created works, a monstrous force that had to be overcome, in this case by a divine sword that controls rather than kills Behemoth.

Behemoth is not destroyed but survives wherever the chaos waters are apparent in creation, whether that be in flourishing swamps or raging rivers. This primordial force remains under El's control, as if Behemoth were a monster who could have his nose pierced with hooks.

Job, a brother of Behemoth, need no longer rage like a chaos monster!

Challenge to Domesticate Leviathan

Job is also challenged to capture and domesticate the chaos monster Leviathan in a manner similar to El's subjugation of Behemoth. However, the capture of a mythic chaos monster with traditional fishing and hunting techniques is futile for humans.

Even if, by an extraordinary feat, Job did capture Leviathan, he could never domesticate him to the point where he became a trusted servant. With a measure of absurd satirical humor, God asks whether Job could transform Leviathan, a chaos monster, into a household pet who would play with Job's children.

In the background may lie the satire found in Psalm 104, where in the context of the vast seas created as God's works of Wisdom, Leviathan is ultimately identified as a monster YHWH transforms into a creature to "play with" as if he were a cosmic toy (Ps 104:26).

The Silencing of Leviathan

Job is again summoned to face the ferocious monster called Leviathan. He is so ferocious that no human has the capacity to face him. If that is so, how can Job dare to imagine standing in the face of the God whom Job described as ferocious and full of terrors. YHWH may well be alluding to Job's earlier hope of standing before God's face, a possibility that is ludicrous if Job cannot even "face" Leviathan.

This YHWH claims to have silenced the boasting of Leviathan and his powerful case before God. Such a claim seems to imply that if YHWH could silence the words of such a ferocious monster, Job would have no chance of confronting God with his words and his case against God. The focus here is not on the primordial Leviathan myths but on the implied comparison of Job with a chaos monster.

The Overwhelming Terrors of Leviathan

In the remainder of this discourse, the narrator indulges in a grand poetic portrayal of Leviathan that must leave Job bewildered and wondering. The spectacular portrait of this mythic monster includes teeth surrounded with terror, a coat of interlocking metal shields, sneezes of flashing lightning, flames of fire leaping from his mouth, smoke emerging from his nostrils, a breath that ignites coals, a face before which dread dances, a heart cast in stone, a crashing presence that terrifies gods, a body that no sword or spear can penetrate, a presence that laughs at weapons of war, a mighty force that terrifies even the Deep, and a mythic power that no one can dominate.

Leviathan is portrayed as the apparently invincible terrifying lord of chaos, a monster who epitomizes the mystery of the primordial, the final consciousness that the therapist stirs in Job's inner being. What follows, in pointed contrast, is Job's brief response (42:1–6), the epitome of a healing experience.

The Wisdom Therapist, after having awakened Job's cosmic consciousness (ch. 38) and Job's Wisdom consciousness (ch. 39), seems to have meandered into a primordial world of mythology that does not seem immediately relevant. If, however, we recognize that this detour may also awaken Job's primordial consciousness, we may realize that cosmic consciousness may connect Job, and other trauma sufferers, with dimensions of the cosmos that are primordial—or in contemporary terms, evolutionary.

CHAPTER 23

Job's Wisdom Healing Experience

Job 42

> *To discern innate Wisdom*
> *active in all the domains*
> *of the universe*
> *is to "see" the dynamic Presence of*
> *Wisdom*
> *permeating the cosmos,*
> *and in the process*
> *to "see" God.*

THE INTERRELATED CONTEXT of Job 42, the epilogue of the book of Job, includes the prologue of chapters 1–2, the specific challenges of the voice from the whirlwind in Job 38:1–3, the exploration of the cosmos in Job 38–39, and the divine encounter with Behemoth and Leviathan in the immediately preceding chapters.

In the healing process, led by the Wisdom Therapist, the function of Job as an adversary is finally dismissed. In the therapy process, Job's therapist has stirred Job's cosmic consciousness, his Wisdom consciousness, and finally his primordial consciousness. He has experienced his world and his new sense of divine presence from radically new perspectives.

Accordingly, it is now possible for Job to respond to this presence, not as an angry adversary, but as a humble human ready to answer his Wisdom Therapist and enunciate the radical change that has occurred in his understanding of reality. Job can now announce that he has been healed.

The narrator, it would seem, has his Wisdom community answer their old covenant God through the person of Job with a bold word of healing consistent with the Wisdom thinking of its cosmic Wisdom God, after the community dismisses its conflict with the Covenant God of the postexilic Israelite community.

He then has Job, and presumably the distressed community, receive a blessing, not because they have confessed any wrong, but because they have discerned the truth about a world governed by Wisdom, their means of discerning a profound spiritual cosmic Presence.

Healing Climax

The opening verses of Job 42 are not only the climax of Job's speeches, but portray, in very succinct form, a declaration that reflects Job's healing, the moment when his trauma is overcome. To appreciate this profound declaration, we need to focus on six features of this speech that each encapsulate a pivotal dimension of this healing event.

Concession: *I know you can do anything, and that no scheme of yours can be thwarted* (v. 2).

Job acknowledges that God has the power to execute any plan he chooses in the "scheme" of the cosmos, a power Job discerned in his tour of the cosmos (in Job 38). Job, however, does not reflect any longer on the cruel "schemes" that Job once believed God was planning to make his life miserable. God trauma is no longer an issue.

Discernment: *Who is this who obscures my design without knowledge? Indeed, I has spoken without discernment, of things **beyond** me which I did not know* (v. 3).

The Wisdom Therapist's questions about the "design" of the cosmos are fundamental to Job's exploration of the cosmos in Job 38. Job's response is a public recognition that his discernment does not match that of this God and that as a result he has "obscured" God's cosmic design with ignorant accusations that lacked his discernment of cosmic Wisdom.

Job also concedes that there are "things beyond him," that is, marvels that are beyond human comprehension (cf. 9:10; 37, 5, 14) but which point to innate cosmic Wisdom as the ordering principle, the "design" of the universe.

Job admits he does not possess cosmic Wisdom that his goal was not the quest for Wisdom but for the presence of God in court. Job's claim that God used Wisdom to traumatize Job is no longer an issue (cf. 12:13–15).

God's Challenge: *You said, "Hear now and I will speak, I will ask, and you will inform me"* (v. 4).

Verse 4 is another quote that Job remembers from the initial challenge of the voice from the whirlwind. In his challenge, Job is expected to accompany this God through the cosmos and answer the Wisdom mysteries found in the domains of the universe. Here Job recognizes that this God is the Wisdom Therapist confronting him with levels of knowledge beyond human capacity to grasp.

Seeing God? This verse (v. 5) has long been the subject of endless debate. Job claims that: *I have heard about you with my ears, but now my eyes "see" you!*

Obviously, Job, as a wise man of the ancient world, has long "heard" about God, from his friends and community. But what does he mean by claiming that "his eyes now see you"? I would argue that this expression is not a metaphor or mystical image. Job claims to "see" God . . . where, how, when?

We first need to recognize that "see" (*ra'a*) is a technical word in the Wisdom tradition and refers to the act of "observing" to discern the Wisdom of a situation (Habel 2015, 14). Earlier this God, as the Wisdom Scientist, searched to the ends of the Earth to "see/observe" where Wisdom was found. And this God "saw" her (28:27). Does Job see God when he sees Wisdom?

If Wisdom can be seen in the cosmos, then apparently so can this God. Seeing Wisdom is tantamount to seeing God! Job does not see God in his imagination, in his mind, or in his spirit. He "sees" God by observing the wonders of Wisdom in the universe. This God is the discernible presence of cosmic Wisdom permeating the domains of the cosmos, not a divine being in the celestial assemblies of heaven.

In a roundabout way, Job has achieved his goal to meet God, not as his adversary in court but as the Wisdom Presence in the design of the cosmos. To see God as Wisdom Presence in the cosmos overcomes his sense of God as the Seeing Eye observing him down on Earth. God can be "seen" in the domains and design of the cosmos, not necessarily as a discrete celestial being but as a Wisdom force that integrates, permeates, and activates the universe.

Retraction: The final verse in Job's final response incorporates two actions that reveal that Job's trauma has terminated and that he is healed. He declares: *Therefore I retract and change my mind about dust and ashes* (v. 6).

Earlier YHWH had recognized Job as the one with a "lawsuit against Shaddai" (40:2). "Seeing" God as the cosmic presence of Wisdom is sufficient vindication for Job of YHWH's integrity. Job therefore decides not to "answer" and press his suit but to "retract" his case. Job does not negate the words he has spoken but withdraws his case against his former God. The court case trauma is over!

Healing: Job's final words are also often debated. In my translation, Job declares he has changed his mind about living with "dust and ashes." Some translations suggest that Job "repents in dust and ashes," a rendition that suggests Job finally confesses his wrong. Nothing could be further from the truth.

"Dust and ashes" may refer back to 2:8 where Job's friends found him lying in misery. They represent his status as a humiliated human suffering extreme trauma. And while the verb *nacham* may be rendered "repent," it also means "change one's mind." Job has not only changed his mind about pursuing litigation but also chosen to abandon his world of misery and get on with life. Job's change of mind is not an inner act of repentance but an announcement of his new status as a healed hero.

YHWH's Verdict

Ironically, this YHWH does not pronounce a verdict on Job during his case against God, but only after Job has withdrawn his suit, and then only indirectly by rebuking Job's friends. Amazingly, YHWH announces that Job's bold accusations in his speeches are free from blame. Job is not damned for screaming at God. His accusations may in fact be closer to the truth than the pronouncements of the friends. Job's screams were closer to reality, to the naked "truth."

Ironically, the friends who demanded Job plead for God's mercy because they believed he was a sinner now find themselves in need of Job's intercession. Job is now called to play the role of priest as he once did for his family (1:5). Job is reinstated as a mediator even before his family is restored. Job had previously yearned for an arbiter or redeemer to handle his case with God.

Now Job, healed of his God trauma, becomes the mediator. There is healing not only with God but also with his community of friends.

YHWH's Blessing

The narrator announces YHWH's blessing before outlining the details. Job's restoration, in the context of the dialogue with his friends, is clearly an act of grace, not a reward from a righteous God for Job's integrity or achievements as a hero.

The belated act of "consoling" and "comforting" Job is an ironic reminder of these same functions performed by his friends without success from the beginning of his period of trauma (2:11). His friends even give Job *qesita*, pieces of silver, and a gold ring.

Job is blessed by all parties, even YHWH, who restores his fortune twofold and extends his life an additional hundred and forty years, twice the normal lifespan. He is of the same vintage as the patriarchs and worships El, the same God. Job dies "healed" and happy, "sated with days."

BIBLIOGRAPHY

Balentine, Samuel. 2008. "Traumatising Job." *Rev Exp* 105: 213–228.

Baldwin, Jennifer. 2018. *Trauma-Sensitive Theology: Thinking Theologically in the Era of Trauma*. Eugene, OR: Cascade Books.

Boase, Elizabeth. 2016. "Fragmented Voices: Collective Identity and Traumatization in Lamentations." In *Bible through the Lens of Trauma*, edited by Elizabeth Boase and Christopher Frechette, 49–65. Atlanta, GA: SBL Press.

———. 2017. "Whispered in the Sound of Silence." *The Bible and Critical Theory* 12, no. 1: 4–22.

Boase, Elizabeth, and Christopher Frechette, eds. 2016. *The Bible through the Lens of Trauma*. Atlanta, GA: SBL.

Frechette, Christopher, and Elizabeth Boase. 2016. "Defining Trauma as a Useful Lens for Biblical Interpretation." In *Bible through the Lens of Trauma*, edited by Elizabeth Boase and Christopher Frechette, 1–23. Atlanta, GA: SBL Press.

Garber, David. 2015. "Trauma Theory and Biblical Studies." *Currents in Biblical Studies* 14: 24–44.

Gray, John. 1957. *The Legacy of Canaan*. Leiden, Netherlands: E. J. Brill.

Guerrero, Corinna. 2015. "Encountering Trauma in the Bible." *The Living Word*, October: 1–8.

Habel, Norman. 1977. "Only the Jackal is My Friend: On Friends and Redeemers in Job." *Interpretation* 31: 227–236.

———.1985. *The Book of Job: A Commentary*. Philadelphia, PA: Westminster Press.

———.2001. "Is the Wild Ass Willing to Serve You? Challenging the Mandate to Dominate." In *The Earth Bible III*, edited by Norman Habel, 179–189. Sheffield: Sheffield Academic Press.

———. 2008. *Exploring Ecological Hermeneutics*. Atlanta, GA: Society of Biblical Literature.

———. 2014. *Finding Wisdom in Nature: An Ecological Reading of the Book of Job*. Sheffield: Sheffield Phoenix Press.

———. 2015. *Discerning Wisdom in God's Creation: Following the Way of Ancient Scientists*. Melbourne: Morning Star Publishing.

———. 2021. *The Wisdom Trinity*. Adelaide: ATF.

Helsel, Philip Browning. 2016. "Sacred Pleasure to Soothe the Broken Spirit: Collective Trauma and Qoheleth." In *The Bible through the Lens of Trauma*, edited by Elizabeth Boase and Christopher Frechette. Atlanta, GA: SBL.

Houck-Loomis, Tiffany. 2018. *History through Trauma and Counter-History in the Hebrew Bible*. Eugene, OR: Wipf & Stock.

Hunsinger, Deborah van Deusen. 2015. *Bearing the Unbearable: Trauma, Gospel, and Pastoral Care*. Cambridge: Eerdmans.

Janzen, David. 2012. *The Violent Gift: Trauma's Subversion of the Deuteronomistic History's Narrative*. New York: T & T Clark.

Kleinman, A. 1986. *Social Origins of Distress and Disease. Depression, Neurasthenia, and Pain in Modern China*. New Haven, CT: Yale University Press.

Lacocque, Andre. 2007. "The Deconstruction of Job's Fundamentalism." *JBL* 126, no. 1 (Spring): 83–97.

Newsom, Carol. 2003. *The Book of Job: A Contest of Moral Imaginations*. Oxford: Oxford University Press.

Raheb, Mitri. 2014. *Faith in the Face of Empire: The Bible through Palestinian Eyes*. Maryknoll, NY: Orbis Books.

Ruprecht, E. 1971. "Das Nilpferd in Hiochbuch." *Vetus Testamentum* 21: 209–231.

Smith Landsman, Irene. 2002. "Crisis of Meaning in Trauma and Loss." In *Loss of the Assumptive World: A Theory of Traumatic Loss*, edited by Jeffrey Kauffman, 10–20. New York: Brunner-Routledge.

West, Gerald. 2016. "Between Text and Trauma: Reading Job with People Living with HIV." In *Bible through the Lens of Trauma*, edited by Elizabeth Boase and Christopher Frechette, 209–230. Atlanta, GA: SBL Press.